WITHDRAWN

THE VIOLENT FAMILY

THE VIOLENT FAMILY

Victimization of Women, Children and Elders

Nancy Hutchings, M.S.W.

Southern Connecticut State University
New Haven, Connecticut

HUMAN SCIENCES PRESS, INC.
72 FIFTH AVENUE
NEW YORK, N.Y. 10011-8004

Printed in the United States of America
987654321

Library of Congress Cataloging in Publication Data

The Violent family.

　　Includes bibliographies and index.
　　　1.　Family violence—United States.　2.　Family violence
—Law and legislation—United States.　I.　Hutchings, Nancy.
[DNLM: 1.　Child Abuse.　2.　Family.　3.　Spouse
Abuse.　4.　Violence.　HQ 809.3 V795]
HQ809.3.U5V58 1988　　　　　　　362.8 ' 2　　　　　　87-3812
ISBN 0-89885-383-4

CONTENTS

CONTRIBUTORS

Nancy Hutchings, M.S.W., A.C.S.W.   Associate Professor, Social Work, Southern Connecticut State University. Doctoral Candidate at New York University, School of Public Administration.

Edward Mallarkey, J. Harvard Law School.   Assistant State's Attorney, Division of Criminal Justice, State of Connecticut.

Margaret Martin, M.S.W., A.C.S.W.   Assistant Professor, Elms College, Chicopee, Mass. Doctoral Student, Heller School, Brandeis University. Formerly Director Victim, Offender and Battered Women's Program, Danielson, Connecticut.

Barbara Moynihan, R.N., M.S., N.C.S.   Clinical Specialist in Adult Psychiatric Nursing, Private Practitioner, Director of New Haven Rape Crisis Services, Y.W.C.A. of Greater New Haven. Doctoral Candidate at University of Connecticut.

Julia Hamilton, M.S.W., A.C.S.W.   Assistant Professor, Department of Pediatrics, Yale Medical School, Chief Social Worker, Primary Care Center and Emergency Room, Yale-New Haven Hospital, Associate Professor at Southern Connecticut State University. Doctoral candidate at Yeshiva University, School of Social Work.

Donna Waldron DiGioia, M.S. in Research and Quantitative Analysis, Southern Connecticut State University; Extensive research on pornography and violence.

Frank O'Connor, M.S.W., A.C.S.W.   Instructor, Social Work Medicine, Yale Medical School, Staff Social Worker, Department of Social Work, Yale-New Haven Hospital.

9

PREFACE

In studying family life in the United States in the 1980s, one becomes aware of the increase of violence in the family and crimes of violence on the street. This book attempts to explain some of the causes of family violence. These are discussed in Chapters 1 and 2. The legal system is set forth in Chapter 3 by Edward Mullarkey, a State's Attorney in Connecticut, whose particular interest is the court's approach to victims of family violence.

Margaret Martin, a social worker, reviews the legal system as she has experienced it with victims of violence. In Chapter 5 she also discusses the problems of battered women, exploring some of the causes of this form of violence, of which, in recent years, the media has made the American public much more keenly aware.

This book encourages readers to sustain their alertness to child abuse in its various forms, and a pediatric social worker from Yale-New Haven Hospital, Julia Hamilton, includes case examples and current theories of violence against children in her Chapter 6.

A newly surfacing form of family violence—"Granny-Bashing"—is coming to the attention of doctors, nurses, and social workers. With many families now caring for elderly relatives, the stress and pressures may result in abuse of the elderly. Frank O'Connor, a social worker from Yale-New Haven Hospital, analyzes this new dynamic in Chapter 7.

Rape is of course not necessarily only a crime of violence in the family; but it has a profound effect on family members, and often occurs within the family unit or among close friends; therefore Chapter 8, by Barbara Moynihan, nurse-director of a Rape Crisis Center, is included in this context. The very theories that apply to rape are applicable in cases of child abuse and wife-battering.

Chapter 9, on the pervasiveness of pornography, is offered as a further effort in this volume to scrutinize the causes of family violence. Certainly no one factor can be labeled as primary; but the upsurge in violence in the media and in the culture that surrounds us in the 1980s is a primary fact of life.

It is the hope of the editor and the contributing authors that this book will foster a fuller understanding of family violence and of what it means to be a victim.

Nancy Hutchings

ACKNOWLEDGMENTS

A special thanks to Barbara Moynihan of The New Haven Rape Crisis Center for her help in getting this book together. I also want to thank Maggie, Julia, Frank, Ed, and Donna for their hard work and personal support.

President Michael Adanti, of Southern Connecticut State University, and the Professional Development Support Committee were most helpful with typing services. A special thanks to Jean Alberino, whose rescue efforts were most appreciated.

And last, but not least, to all the students over the years who have given me encouragement, and who make teaching worthwhile.

Chapter 1

INTRODUCTION

In the world today, bombings, hijackings, and terrorism are "normal"; yet in the United States, the scene of most of the violence is the home. In fact, the American home is considered more violent than any other national setting other than the military.[1]

Other countries are known for their civil wars, their acts of murder and terrorism; our country is considered peaceful. But it is the households in the United States that are dangerous. On the domestic front there is violence between spouses, between siblings, between parents and children and, most recently, toward the grandparents who are often living in the home. Violence is self-perpetuating so that once it is accepted in a family as a means of communication or as punishment, it is hard to terminate. Violence becomes accepted as normal family behavior.

The statistics in the 1980s on domestic violence often seem overwhelming. Yet, according to most experts, wife battering, rape, and child abuse are still crimes that often are not reported to the authorities, so that the statistics are understatements.

It was not until 1968 that all states mandated the reporting of child abuse. Even with this mandate, many cases go unreported because different localities and different agencies hold different criteria for "abuse." Also, of course individuals (teachers, nurses, social workers, etc.) do the reporting, so that their personal feelings on what and whom they report can widely differ.

BACKDROP TO VIOLENCE

The conviction that severe physical discipline was indispensable to child rearing has been prevalent for centuries. By parents, guardians, and teachers, children were punished with canes, rods, and whips. In a well-known text, the Bible exhorted, "Thou shalt beat him with rods and thou shalt save his soul from hell." Theology continued to support severe punishment of children. By the doctrine of original sin, children were born corrupt, and parents were to beat the Devil out of them. The prestige of "thy father and thy mother" was unassailable. Although his health was shattered in childhood by his father's brutality, the writer Anton Chekhov cherished the old man. The late nineteenth century, from Chekhov's Russia to the England of Charles Dickens and Samuel Butler, is a chronicle of child abuse.

These same theories permeate historical and religious tradition regarding violence toward women. For many centuries, a husband was legally allowed to beat his wife. The phrase "rule of thumb" referred to the English Common law that sanctioned a husband striking his wife providing the switch was no thicker than the thumb.[2]

Violence between spouses seems to be on the increase or, certainly, it is being reported more often. Historically, a man's home was his castle and he was given the right to privacy for his behavior. Since up until the late nineteenth century, it was legally permissible to beat his wife, many people still tacitly accept this behavior. Historically, the first law of marriage proclaimed by the Romans was that married women were to conform themselves to the temper of their husbands and husbands could rule them as though they were possessions.[3] The husband was given the legal right to control his wife. The biblical King Ahasuerus deposed his queen (Esther's predecessor) when she refused to appear at his drunken orgy, lest her rebellion undermine the authority of husbands. Even with Christianity, the hierarchy of the family with the man as the head of the household, with all the authority, was continued. By the biblical account, Eve—the Maker's after-thought—was created from Adam's rib. Over the centuries the subordinate status of women was reinforced so that legally they had no rights against beatings or cruel punishment. Students of the early history of witchcraft have often concluded that it was the strong and independent women in the community who were labelled as the deviants.

Since the legal systems in Europe, England, and early colonial times in the United States supported the husband's right to beat his wife, it is very difficult to bring about a complete change in thinking. In 1964 in the U.S. a woman was killed in the street and bystanders did not interfere because it was a dispute between a husband and wife,[4] though by that date it was against the law for a husband to beat his wife. Due to the women's suffrage movement, by 1910 most states granted divorce to women with proof of physical cruelty.

THE HOME: A TRAINING SCHOOL FOR VIOLENCE

A study conducted by Straus, Gelles, and Steinmetz in the late 1970s, revealed startling statistics. One out of six wives are beaten each year. Three out of five parents use physical punishment with their children, and one out of two families is a scene of domestic violence each year. This study used 2,143 families which the researchers chose as a representative sample of the total population. At least one out of every three married couples seems to accept the idea that it is permissible to hit their spouse. According to many husbands and wives, the marriage license gives permission for violence. A high majority of parents, over 75 percent, approved of violence as a legitimate form of training for children. Of the 46 million children in the United States in 1975 (census 1975) it was estimated by this study that between 3 to 4 million children were kicked, bitten, or punched at some time in their lives.[5] Punishment thus is not limited to slapping or spanking.

Since violent households virtually constitute a norm in the United States, how can we prevent these children from becoming violent adults? The Straus study reflects wide acceptance of physical violence, especially towards children. It is therefore not surprising that we are seeing more violence in schools and on the streets. The American home often is a training school for violence. The study not only demonstrated that children who were physically punished not only abused their own children, since that was the model set for them, they also showed a higher rate of hitting their spouses. "Each generation learns to be violent by being a participant in a violent family."[6]

In studying violent families, many professionals assumed that lower-class families were the chief culprits. Police calls and visits to emergency care in hospitals might substantiate this; but the study by Straus supported the belief of feminist scholars that child abuse and wife battering pervades all economic levels. It is possible that middle-income families, with more intense financial pressures, have more family stress, which results in violence in the home. The husband under stress at his job unleashes his rage at home against his wife and children.

Yet why, basically, are women and children the victims of violence? Violence is seen by many as a means to control others, to exert power, and to legitimize the roles of family members.

SEX-ROLE STEREOTYPING

Developmental psychologists have encouraged stereotyping of men and women since the early 1900s. The developmental theories that are taught to all professionals, doctors, nurses, teachers, and social workers, have been based on Freud's view of psychosexual development. The man has the superior body and is active and aggressive in his sexual role; the woman is passive and receptive in hers. Freud's theories suggested that women even became masochistic because they felt so inferior.[7] For many psychologists, this theory translated into the theme that women received sexual pleasure from beatings. Many authors have referred to Freud's theory of penis envy as meant to dominate a woman's behavior.

According to Freud, women showed a lesser sense of justice than men and were more influenced by their feelings when making judgments.[8] Erickson's theories of psychosocial development echo this when he refers to the "inner" sphere of female development. A woman's identity, which is essential in Erickson's thinking, is difficult to establish for it "is internal, inaccessible and diffuse."[9] Her ambivalence toward her reproductive system causes her search for identity to be delayed and to be much more complex than the masculine search for identity.

Are men and women really different psychologically? Is anatomy responsible for the destiny of each of us? Do the gender types described in Broverman's study hold true?[10] Margaret Mead has presented studies of different tribes where the men are more nurturing or where both sexes are equally aggressive in warlike behavior. Her studies proved again that sexual roles are determined and reinforced by different cultures.[11]

Treating boys and girls in a different way from their earliest years establishes their identities as different. Children's socialization begins in the home and continues at school. The earliest role model for the girl is the nurturant female, her mother; and the mother treats the male child in a different manner. His role model is individualized by the earliest parent figures. Boy children are often allowed by parents to be more demanding and to expect service from the female, either their mother or their siblings. Many cultures make very obvious their preference for male children.

In cultures in Asia and India female children have been put to death because they could not contribute as much productivity in a agrarian economy where the food is scarce. Children are trained in their sexual roles according to the requirements of their particular cultures. Economy then has something to do with the stereotyping of females. More complex industrial societies do have more diffuse gender role expectations. That should be the prime reason for discontinuing stereotyping in American society today. Sixty percent of women in the United States are working, yet they are not making the contributions that are most needed nor are they living up to their fullest potential.

Yet women, who are mothers, are the primary socializers; they set the feminine role model for their daughters and by individualizing and treating their male children in a different fashion, they are establishing the different masculine role model. The female child is encouraged to follow the mother's role; she is easily led to her gender role model. But the male child must be something different from the very beginning; he is given more of a challenge.[12] Many people question boys early in life about their career choices.

This challenges them to think of themselves in terms of production, earning money, and as having different goals than females. In today's world this same challenge is still not presented to girls in terms of career choices and future plans. The role of wife, mother, and housekeeper is always implied. It is also obvious to the girl that there is a lesser value placed on her homemaking mother's career than on her father's. There is no pay for housework; the work is often servile, with little appreciation shown.

For this to change, men must be brought up differently. There is too much pressure on the male child to produce at a high economic level in a very complex society and there still is not enough economic challenge to the female children. Boys are afraid of career failure and many adolescent girls are afraid to be too successful academically or in their careers. They are afraid to succeed. Many successful career women fear that they will lose their "feminine appeal" if they become too successful. Matina Horner's study indicated that many college women had a "motive to avoid success."[13] The "motive" was a fear of loss of their feminine appeal for men. Rosabeth Moss Kanter, writing about women who became successful executives in large corporations, describes the many compromises and difficulties that challenge them. For all the obstacles they surmount, "tokenism" seems to explain those few who succeed.[14]

Where does society get its image of the successful woman? Advertising has a strong psychological effect in defining proper feminine role. Women clean house, they are mothers, and they are sexual partners. They are programmed by the media to be concerned about their appearance; men are programmed or even brainwashed to believe that physical beauty is paramount in a woman.

> Madison Avenue Woman is a combination sex object and wife and mother who achieves fulfillment by looking beautiful and alluring for boyfriends and lovers and cooking, cleaning, washing, or polishing for her husband and family. She is not very bright; she is submissive and subservient to men; if she has a job, it is probably that of a secretary or an airline hostess.[15]

It is interesting that both of these careers often shown in advertising are those that have her waiting on men. Women routinely appear as sex objects in advertisements. Who can buy a whiskey, a cigarette, or an automobile without having a lovely woman to sell it to them? Advertising strongly reinforces society's concepts about male and female roles. The sex-role stereotypes would not be so acceptable to advertisers if they had not already accepted them as valid.

There are other reinforcements of stereotyping in our society; the textbooks used in schools, romance novels, and our most popular television programs such as *Dallas* or *Dynasty*, all establish this position more firmly. Women are sex objects the most often; occasionally, in the 1980s, they are allowed to follow male careers such as police officer or be television and newspaper reporters. Still, the working women who are most often portrayed on television are secretaries, waitresses, or in some secondary position. The women who seem to have wealth and power are still dependent on their male partners for their positions and their status.

The ideas that men and women develop as to who they are, how they relate to each other, and what futures they both should have are dependent on cultural factors. Society conveys messages, images, as to what a woman should be and what a man should be. This image reduces a woman to a secondary position and causes her to devalue herself. Women and men should be thought of in terms of equality as humans so that early images given to children can be more adrogynous. There should never *be* an article entitled "Wives: The 'Appropriate' Victims of Marital Violence."[16] Obviously, no one is ever "appropriate" for violence; but sexism and stereotyping have fostered the idea that violence towards women and children is acceptable.

Are mental health professionals trained to help victims of violence in the family? What happens to women who come to psychotherapists or social work agencies with problems in their family? As was noted, traditional theories of psychosocial development were based on Freudian and Neo-Freudian theories. The psychologically "normal" woman was concerned chiefly with her roles as a wife and as a mother. Women were defined, and often defined themselves, in terms of their *roles in a family*. They were not encouraged to verbalize their individual personalities, leaving out their families. What were *their* goals? Their unfulfilled desires?

Inge Broverman did a study of 79 clinically trained psychologists, psychiatrists, and social workers (both men and women) to ask them to label characteristics as masculine, feminine, and those of the healthy mature adult. The masculine traits closely paralleled those labeled as mentally healthy for *all* adults. These characteristics, labeled masculine, included: competent, independent, rational, and logical.[17]

If clinicians have accepted a negative stereotyping about women and mental health, how can they be supportive and enhance the ego strengths of those women who come to them from violent and abusive marriages? The Freudian philosophy that women are masochistic and feel inferior seems to permeate the working of many clinical therapists. Phyllis Chesler believes that clinicians treat women patients as children and assume that being a wife and mother will bring mental health. She feels that the patriarchal therapist-patient relationship simply duplicates the unhappy marriages of many females.[18] Since many women who come to psychotherapists (psychiatrists, psychologists, or social workers) are trying to establish their own identities, the old value system of sex stereotyping and male domination will not offer a cure.

The history of social work is based on a strong feminist movement. The leading figures in social work at the turn of the century and into the 1920s were women. They were women who pressed for reforms such as child labor laws, better working conditions for women, and improvement of housing in the crowded cities. They were the founders of the first settlement houses. The first school of social work was established because a woman staff member in the Charity Organization Society presented a paper calling for a national training school in applied philanthropy.[19] This was in 1897. Mary Richmond, the first social work professional, also wrote the first textbook used in training professionals.[20] The progressive movement for reforms in the field of social welfare was led by women in the early 1900s.

However, in the 1920s and 1930s, Sigmund Freud was the dominant influence in the training of social workers. Psychosocial treatment, with its assumptions about the ego capacities of males and females, was the most influential theory in training social workers. According to Freudian theory,[21] environment and cultural influences had little impact on individuals. Freud supported a patriarchal viewpoint of the family, and his theories supported one explanation for violence in the family.

During the Depression, concern rose for the disadvantaged and the oppressed, and social workers actively supported Roosevelt's reforms in social legislation. They also were active in the Civil Rights Movement in the 1960s. Yet somehow the profession has never considered women as a collective group of clients. Traditional family service agencies still seem to focus on women's roles as wives and mothers in establishing causes for mental health problems. A Yale psychiatrist published a book in 1984 claiming that the women's liberation movement has increased anxieties and depression in women.[22] The movement actually has freed many of them to go to agencies for help; but the professionals are often not equipped to help them.

A NEW AWARENESS

The 1970s did bring the women's movement to a leadership position in the United States. Shelters were opened for battered wives, awareness of physical and sexual abuse of children proliferated the media and mandated reporting laws for such abuse were passed in all states. Yet professional social workers with traditional middle-class values have not been very active in women's agencies. The leadership has come from the grass roots feminist leaders in each community. Some social workers claim it is because men hold the leadership positions in the profession and thus the power. Others believe that it is too painful or threatening for women to face child abuse and battered wives, for we identify too closely with the victims.

Whatever those reasons, it is essential to train future social workers so that awareness of violence in the family permeates their clinical thinking. Recognizing the wide prevalence of violence that exists against women and children in the American family is essential to making sound social work assessments in clinics, schools, and family service agencies. The new awareness of the existence of sexual abuse in many families has helped professionals in taking histories in mental health facilities and other social work settings. Keeping open eyes and ears and a willingness to hear is the best way for social workers to begin to comprehend and address the extent of violence in the American home. Various techniques, such as consciousness-raising, group therapy, and individual ego support can help women to conquer the feelings of inadequacy and inferiority that both society and their family relationships have fomented. Social workers are the ideal professionals to work in schools, hospitals, and family service agencies to provide this support needed by women and children. We also should be assuming more leadership positions in shelters and crisis services that specialize in violence against women and children. We hope that the chapters in this book will provide material to encourage our profession to take a stronger position of leadership than it has done to date.

NOTES

1. Straus, M. A., Gelles, R. J., & Steinmetz, K. *Behind closed doors: Violence in the American family.* Garden City: Anchor Press, 1980, p. 4.
2. Martin, D. *Battered wives.* New York: Pocket Books, 1976, p. 32.
3. Dobash, R. E., & Dobash, R. P. Wives: The "appropriate" victims of marital violence," *Victimology*, 1977–78, 2, p. 427.
4. Straus, M. A., Gelles, J., & Steinmetz, S. K., Kitty Genovese's murder. op. cit. p. 46.
5. Ibid., p. 73.
6. Ibid., p. 121.
7. Wesley, C. The women's movement and psychotherapy. *Social Work*, March 1975, p. 120.
8. Gilligan, C. *In a different voice: Psychological theory and women's development.* Harvard University Press, Cambridge. 1982, p. 7.
9. Bardwick, J., & Douvan, E. Ambivalence: The socialization of women, In Gornick, Vivian, Moran, & Barbara, Eds. - *Woman in sexist society.* New York: Basic Books, 1971, p. 232.
10. Broverman, I., Broverman, D., Clarkson, F., Rosenkrantz, P., & Vogel, S. R. *Readings on the psychology of women.* New York: Harper & Row. 1972, pp. 329–324.

11. Chodorow, N. Being and doing: A crosscultural examination of the socialization of males and females. In *Woman in sexist society.* op. cit. p. 260.
12. Gilligan, C. op. cit. p. 8.
13. Horner, M. S. The motive to avoid success and changing aspirations of college women. In *Readings on the psychology of women.* op. cit. pp. 62–67.
14. Kanter, R. M. *Men and women of the corporation.* New York: Basic Books, 1977.
15. Komisar, L. The image of woman in advertising. In *Woman in sexist society.* op. cit. p. 306.
16. Hunter College. Women's studies collective. *Women's Realities, Women's Choices.* New York: Oxford University Press, 1983, p. 54.
17. Dobash, R. E., & Dobash, R. P. op. cit. p. 426.
18. Broverman, I. et al. op cit. pp. 320–324.
19. Chesler, P. *Women and madness.* New York: Avon, 1972, pp. 73, 74.
20. Brieland, D. Costin, L., & Atherton, C. *Contemporary social work: An introduction to social work and social welfare.* McGraw-Hill. New York 1985, p. 40.
21. Ibid. p. 175.
22. Ibid. p. 142.
23. Okpaku, S. *Sex, orgasm and depression: Their inter-relationship in a changing society.* New Haven, CT: Chrisolith Books, 1984.

Chapter 2

THE ECONOMIC STATUS OF WOMEN IN THE UNITED STATES

Nancy Hutchings

JOBS BY GENDER

Control over economic resources is a key source of power in all industrialized nations. There are public and private institutions within our society where that power is exercised. Laws, social policies, and physical forcefulness tend to give the male members in society more power than the females. Also, the corporate institutions in America are controlled by masculine leaders; they therefore control the use of economic resources. Even in the career opportunities that are considered female, nursing, education, and social work, men occupy the leadership positions that decide the policies on wages, promotions, and hiring.

It is ruinous to women that gender is a criterion for the assignment of work. With the Industrial Revolution came a new division of labor. Men and women were not sharing the tasks equally as they had in the agrarian economy. The man went out to earn a living and the woman stayed home to care for the home and the children. Her roles were defined in terms of the family structure. Some women have exercised considerable power within their families and have certain control over their husbands and children in many areas; but essentially the husband's role as the wage earner gives him more power, undergirded by social, religious, and legal sanctions.

The wife's sphere of control is very circumscribed. The violence in many families occurs when the husband does not feel he has enough power and control at his job or in the community and then abuses his power with his wife and children. Human beings need to feel that they are in control somewhere, and men have been socialized to believe that aggression is acceptable for themselves. It is inevitable that violence will result, so long as society accepts it.

As earlier noted, women in the United States often continue to be defined in relation to their family roles rather than their economic or political status. Women now constitute 45 percent of the total civilian work force.[1] To stress their roles as housewives therefore is irrelevant. With the feminist movement has also come a push to recognize the value that domestic work should be accorded. Laws have been introduced that state that housework should be covered by Social Security benefits. A study by Chase Manhattan Bank revealed that the average housewife works 99.6 hours each week combining housework and the other family tasks of shopping, chauffeuring, and doing chores for her husband and children.[2] Yet housewives who become disabled are not covered by any program, nor do they receive retirement benefits. The federal government, when it designed the Social Security system, calculated women homemakers in terms of their dependent role in relation to a husband. Housework is a labor that is bought and sold in the economy and working wives often pay for this assistance at home. Wives, who are not paid, are still told there is little calculable value to what they do, it is a "labor of love." The power that a husband gains from controlling the flow of money into the family would be lessened if he paid his wife for her services. Again, social and political theories concede that power comes with the control of money and property, and in our society, this control still primarily belongs to the males. For women to gain true economic equality with men would involve sacrifice of male comfort and convenience, and of a support to male egos that has been the "natural" male prerogative for centuries. Change therefore will not come easily.[3] Aristocrats did not want the working classes to have more power; whites have resisted the minority groups gaining new economic strength; and women would be the largest group of all ever to gain economic equality.

Because women produce and nurture the young, it has been assumed that they are limited in their abilities to participate in a productive economy. When women first went into factories, it was believed that they did not have the physical strength to do hard manual labor. Lifting young children and pushing furniture should prove the opposite. It would be more truthful to admit that women's reproductive roles provide rationalizations, not reasons, to exclude them from certain jobs. Men hope that women will stay within the family structure, filling their reproductive role which provides the next generation of essential laborers. Yet the problem of the 1980s is that women have not stayed in the home and that the economic marketplace is not giving them the equality or the power that is their entitlement.

HISTORIC FORCES

With the Industrial Revolution and the growth of urban areas, men migrated to the cities and were able to choose from a variety of jobs. Women migrants were attached to men and families or sank to the lowest economic levels in domestic service. In the urban areas, scathing moral judgments were passed on women prostitutes. But for many poor women, it was the only way to survive. As factories and major industries grew in many countries, the need to get cheap labor to increase profits caused the demand for employment of women and children. For centuries, women had received *no* pay for housework, so it was natural for capitalists to offer them low wages. Female factory workers who worked in textile mills throughout New England received half the pay given to men.[4] Many theories have been advanced as to the cause of low pay for women, but it may all originate in the devaluation of housework. Since for centuries, women had received no pay for caring for a house, a husband, and children, it was easy for them to begin with low salaries. In those early years in American factories, the mills and the garment industry were dependent on the low pay scale of women workers.

The Industrial Revolution turned productivity away from the

family and smaller institutions into larger impersonal factories and offices. Increased technical specialization created division of labor, and maintenance and secondary positions were developed to keep productivity in highest gear. Women were allowed in these supportive secondary positions.

Such other career opportunities as opened for women grew from an extension of their domestic roles. The first area of big demand was education. The nurturing roles of mother and wife led to the caretaking of school children. This new role for women developed from their natural place in the family structure and from society's need for care for the young.

The other outgrowth of the Industrial Revolution that led to careers for women began with the volunteer movement. The growth of cities and the problems of the poor in the ghetto urban areas led to the development of health and welfare agencies. Women volunteers visited the homes of the poor to bring food and clothing if the wage earner was ill or had died. This began in the late 1800s, and, by the turn of the century, welfare agencies began to pay their women volunteers. They were the first social workers. Since their positions had grown from the unpaid status of volunteering, it was, once again, natural to pay low wages to the first social workers. In the health field, women had volunteered to care for the sick and, as these numbers increased, they too were given low pay as nurses. It is interesting to note that with the increase of health and welfare agencies in the early 1900s, the *staffs* were professional women; but the *board directors* were business*men*, who duly took prudent advantage of the volunteer spirit of women to pay low wages.

Even the paid work given to women early in the twentieth century tended to be of the nurturing-helpmate type that society had always expected of women. Their housewife-mother roles had merely been extended into the larger society when they accepted maintenance or service employment as domestics, nurses, social workers, or secretaries. Women went to work in institutions such as hospitals, schools, churches, or social work agencies, where the presence of men as leaders and employers maintained the paternalistic institutional life,[5] and the atmosphere of male dominance and the need to court male approbation that had been the story of their lives. The low pay given to women in the service professions underscores their lack of real power.

VOLUNTARISM: NICHE OR TRAP?

Feminists argue about the spirit of voluntarism. They feel it exploits women who should be seeking careers and being paid. This certainly was true in the early part of this century. It could be said that voluntarism was responsible for the low pay of the first nurses, social workers, and teachers. It also can be said of the conservative administrations of both Nixon and Reagan that they hoped to substitute voluntarism for government allocations for domestic programs in health and welfare. Another argument offered is that voluntarism is an attempt to keep women out of the competitive market. Many women are ambivalent about accepting employment outside of their own homes, or they may not feel capable or ready for full-time employment. It could be argued that health and welfare agencies are paternalistic and exploit women; or, that they are excellent training grounds for women to gain professional self-confidence. Women are counseled to enter volunteer experience on their resumés. But the key element of a resumé is salary history. The "compassion trap" which starts many women into the service careers is an interesting dilemma. Socialization may cause "a pervasive belief that women's primary and most valuable social function is to provide the tender and compassionate components of life . . ."[6] This compassionate role model may distort the individual identity of many women. It certainly has been fostered within the family structure by the reproductive and nurturing role of women.

This trap did lead many women into the volunteer movement in the early 1900s. Women were encouraged to volunteer so that they would be "fulfilled." Marriage was still the chief career for women; but volunteering was accepted as good training for women, and it was not an economic threat to men. In the early 1900s, women were expected to feel satisfied with the successful performance of cooking, cleaning, and mothering roles. They would bring fulfillment. If women did not choose marriage, the careers of teaching, nursing, or social work (with low wages) offered "satisfaction and security." The choice was between companionship and marriage or solitude and a career with low wages—if that could be called a choice.

Volunteering is no substitute for achievement which comes from the sense of power that economic resources give to a worker. The problem with volunteering for many women is that although they get a sense of "participation," and of being "involved," they have no real sense of *power*, since they have nothing to do with making institutional policies. Women who are paid workers have communication with the administrators, even though they may lack real power; volunteers have nothing. It should be remembered, however, that volunteering has been a transition route for many women to reenter the career world. But governments should never be allowed to invoke the "volunteer spirit" to escape federal and state responsibility for health, education, or welfare funding.[7]

WARTIME CHANGES

During World War I and II it was patriotic for women to go into factories. With men being drafted, armaments manufacturers and other large industrial firms turned to women laborers. Also, women were hired to replace men in the transportation and communication industries. During the First World War, at least 10 million women gained employment.[8] Their entrance into factories was resented by many male workers and by the unions. One source of resentment was that many women, for patriotic or other reasons, were willing to work for less than men. Black women, especially, worked at lower wages, combating both racism and sexism as they left domestic service to enter factory work. Union opposition to female participation has been well documented.[9] It is based on the lower pay for women which threatens *men's* employment; but probably on a deeper fear that women may turn out to be just as qualified. In 1979, only 6.5 million out of 41 million American women workers belonged to labor unions.[10] This lack of membership has caused the union membership to call this the issue of the 1980s for the unions. The unions will have to address the hot issues of wage discrimination, equal opportunity, and sexual harassment before they can truly include women in their membership.

After World War I and during the Depression, women were told that they were taking a job away from "some good man." Employment became unfeminine; women belonged in the home and the kitchen. When World War II came, "Rosie the Riveter" was welcomed back into the factories. Women who had been considered too fragile became riveters, assembly men, draftsmen, and worked wherever they were needed. At the end of the War, women again became physically "unsuited" to such heavy work. Some women still fight for factory and construction jobs; but they meet stiff resistance from male workers and from the unions. Competition for jobs may be one answer. Maintaining the status quo and male power may be another.

WOMEN'S WORK AND WOMEN'S PAY

The professions, many labelled "women's" (nursing, social work, elementary and secondary school teaching and library science) are the lower paying ones and there is a lack of women in the decision-making levels. The "men's" professions such as law, medicine, engineering, and business management all tend to be higher policy-making careers and use women employees in secondary positions. The staff in a hospital is female, yet male doctors or administrators set the policies; female teachers work for male superintendents, and female social workers for male administrators.[11]

Affirmative Action under the Equal Opportunity Act of 1972 is attempting to try to equalize pay and job opportunities, but there still is a tremendous gap between the genders when it comes to wages and opportunities. The federal laws apply only when it can be proven that job specifications for men and women are the same, and legal action takes long periods of time. The problem for women is that most of them are "hired" into jobs that pay the lowest salaries, even though in careers such as nursing and education, the educational requirements may be higher. (Compare a plumber's or an electrician's salary to those of a nurse or a teacher.) The masculine professions are protected by strong labor unions, and the others are considered women's work. The problems of equal pay and opportunities may be improving but basic fundamental changes are needed. The lowest wages in the United States are given to minority women or those recently emigrated to this country who have language handicaps.

Education has been a female profession for years, but not in colleges and universities. They are able to take advantage of women employees because widespread discrimination still exists in the marketplace.

> Institutions that follow "the market" pay markedly different salaries to persons with similar qualifications but of different races or sex. They also pay lower salaries to people in predominantly female fields than they pay those in predominantly male fields having substantially similar requirements of training and ability. For example, predominantly female nursing department faculty get substantially lower pay than faculty in predominantly male pharmacy departments.[12]

The largest proportion of women are in clerical, sales, or service jobs. Even in the selling profession, there is gender selection. Men sell cars, insurance, and large appliances, where salaries and commissions are higher. Women tend to sell clothing, food, cosmetics, and work in stores at lower salaries with no commission.

SEXUAL HARASSMENT

Thirty-five percent of all women in the labor force are in clerical occupations. This is a career where the worker helps to maintain and nurture her boss, usually a male. This can be degrading work and often entails situations of sexual harassment.

Sexual harassment is defined as "any sexually oriented practice that endangers a woman's job—that undermines her job performance and threatens her economic livelihood."[13] This harassment does not have to be obvious or of a physical nature; it may be a verbal innuendo, telling dirty jokes, or making sexual comments to a female worker. All women expect sexual behavior in social situations, but when it is transferred into her office or her workplace, it threatens her economic security. As we have said before, the men have the majority of the power positions even in the female professions, so women are usually in the powerless position when confronting sexual harassment. The traditional response has been that the woman "invites" it; she should be able to "handle it *with dignity.*" Indignity visited upon women thus is parlayed into a kind of opportunity. Once again, a woman is urged to deploy the ultimate feminine trait, and be a "lady."

In a 1976 *Redbook Magazine* survey, of 9,000 readers, 88 percent of the respondents had experienced some form of sexual harassment in the workplace,[14] so it is not a topic to be treated lightly. If women fight back or file complaints, it only seems to worsen their job situations. Male management officers of 1,500 corporations replied to *Harvard Business Review* that they did not feel it was the responsibility of their organizations to change the attitudes of their male employees towards women.[15] Even though women are in the subordinate positions in largely male hierarchical structures, it is still left up to the female employee to handle her own job situations, to fight, to quit, or to be fired.

It does not seem to matter to men if women are in lower level job or top professional positions; all have suffered from sexual harassment in the workplace at some time.[16] Violence against women is usually physical. But harassment on the job is psychological, and it is kept secret and ignored by male administrators. What makes it so important is that a woman loses her job, her financial security, as well as losing self-esteem and confidence. For women who have already been physically victimized before entering the job market, it becomes even more overwhelming. Yet such women often are castigated for "being bitter"—an unfeminine trait.

THE CORPORATE GAME

Since the largest majority of female employees are in clerical positions, what power do they have? According to Rosabeth Moss Kanter, being a secretary can be very limiting. The power and status of a secretary come from the achievements of her boss— not of her own accomplishments. If she is very good at her job, she becomes so invaluable to her boss that he never recommends her promotion for anything higher.[17]

Secretaries are not really part of the hierarchical level structure for executive promotions. They are adjuncts who maintain and nurture their employers. Large corporations are now reaching out for women employees, partly because of equal opportunity laws and affirmative action, but also because so many capable women are graduating from colleges. Yet established corporations discriminate in many ways, sometimes unwittingly. Women are being welcomed into the "bottomless pit of support services," yet are discriminated against at the top.[18]

Harrigan's book, for which the author had talked to hundreds of working women across the United States, stressed that educationally, women are qualified for many management positions in corporations, but they are being denied most of the policy-making positions. Harrigan believes that working in large corporations involves knowing the rules of the game and that the name of the game is office politics. There are rites of passage involved in achieving promotions and white males know the game plan better than females.[19] Corporations are tightly structured, like the armed forces. The competitive aggression that male children are socialized to use helps them to succeed, while women, who are socialized to be more nurturing and sensitive to others' feelings, have not learned to play aggressively. The study of games played by boys and girls[20] refers to women's early socialization to be concerned about the feelings of their playmates when playing competitive sports. This concern hampers them in the business world.

Learning the principle of how to play on a team in the corporate business world is crucial. Once girls become as active as boys in team sports and athletics, they will learn the tricks of locker-room politics. The business world has successfully kept women underpaid. There has been a theory that even in higher positions women *need* less ("their clothes don't cost as much") and will *accept* less; so large corporations have kept female executives at lower salaries. One must mention here that a survey reported in *Business Week* indicated that there are 600 men for every woman in the middle and upper ranks of corporate management.[21] This figure is changing but not at a very fast rate.

What does all this mean for girls and women in the United States today? It means that they still receive lower salaries and have fewer opportunities than men. It means that they are still defined in relation to their *roles in a family*, or in relation to their *nurturing, supportive* "natures." When women enter the workplace, their gender continues to play a *more important part* in their job selection than their race or national origin.[22]

True economic equality for all women will involve considerable sacrifice by men. It has been their natural prerogative for centuries to be in control and have more power. Control over economic resources has been an important part of this control.[23] Improving women's opportunities involves loss of power for men and it also involves a breakdown of the traditional economic structure based on men being the principal wage earners. This structure has been operating for the past 200 years. Women who choose to stay home and raise their families should be paid the salaries that domestics would receive and should be covered by Social Security. Women who go out to work, now 60 percent of all married women, should be paid on an equal basis with men for comparable work.

WOMEN AND PUBLIC ECONOMIC SUPPORT

Since this book is concerned about the women and children who are victims of family violence, it is important to survey the programs available for income maintenance for women. Because of the economic factors already discussed, most women, when left alone, do not have the financial security of personal savings or of jobs with decent salaries. They were previously dependent on their families or a husband for their financial security and that of their children. This is a powerful factor for women faced with battering or child abuse. The issue becomes survival versus survival.

In the history of social welfare, various social institutions have provided help over the centuries for the needy poor. The primary recipients have been the aged, the blind, the disabled, and widows with children. The welfare function has been carried on by the churches, private charities and, often, the extended family. However, in today's industrial society, the role of the extended family has diminished rapidly. It should also be mentioned that the costs of financial support for a woman with children have increased tremendously since the late 1970s. In modern industrial societies, with the decline of the extended family, the federal and state governments have taken over the welfare function. As many as 23 million Americans received some form of public assistance in 1984.[23]

The welfare institution in England and this country has taken many different attitudes toward fatherless children. In the nineteenth century they were placed in institutions and separated from their mother and siblings. Then came the decision in the 1920s and 1930s that local financing by towns and states would keep families together. Residual benefits in the family's own home were less expensive than institutional care. Still, the attitude towards mothers receiving assistance has always been punitive; the assistance is really given for the children ("after all, it's not *their* fault") and is based on the size of the family. The range of monthly benefits in the United States is an average of $91.02 per family in Mississippi to an average of $539 per family in Alaska,[24] where living costs are highest.

There are three major financial programs that affect women and children who are in need of public support—Aid to Families with Dependent Children (AFDC), Supplemental Security Income (SSI), and Old Age, Survivors and Disability Insurance (OASDI or Social Security). The first two programs are means-tested public assistance programs that provide help to those who prove that they have no sources of income and have exhausted all their savings. The amounts receivable are as low as the poverty level of living standard. The theory of low payments is called less eligibility. It is meant to discourage anyone who is physically able to work from applying for public assistance. This theory traces back to the English Poor Laws which sought to punish those who were begging or receiving taxpayers' money.[25] These people were considered the *un*worthy poor and it was hoped that by making public payments so low everyone would be compelled to work, able or not.

When the public and taxpayers evaluate the Social Security program, they consider it to be a worthwhile program. The money received by widows and children or by single women is money contributed by them or their husbands into an insurance program which is used by the dependent, the disabled, or the elderly. Those dependent on these small benefits are considered to be the *worthy* poor. The difficulty with this program is that it is only for the elderly, survivors of deceased workers, the blind, or the disabled; it is not a benefit for young women with children unless they are young widows.

The majority of recipients from any of these programs are women. Nine out of 10 AFDC families are those headed by females; two-thirds of the aged, the disabled, and the blind who are receiving Social Security or SSI are women; and 6 out of 10 aged adults receiving Social Security are women.

The problem for women or children who are victims of violence in a family, or economically dependent for any other reason, is the bureaucracy of public assistance programs. If a woman leaves her husband and applies for public assistance, there is a waiting period to check out her eligibility. To be certified eligible, she *must* have a home, which has passed inspection: but, no landlord will rent to her until *after* she has a down payment. If she has children, an attempt is made to secure child support from the father of the children. When relationships in a family are tense, as is the case with battering husbands or parents who have abused children, the regulations imposed by the public assistance programs are particularly punitive. Since the application for public help occurs during the emergency crisis stage for the family, it would be most beneficial if immediate financial assistance could be awarded. This, taxpayers would *never* permit! Local welfare agencies, often very political, are the usual source for emergency funds.

Another major problem for women with children who are the victims of violence is providing proper child care. Shelters for battered wives are very concerned about the quality of child care that they provide for the children, for the staff members are very aware that these children have had disastrous home lives and need special emotional reassurance. Usually the shelters have special support programs for children at the same time that their mothers are receiving other social work services.

The mother's difficulties in providing child care begin when she leaves the shelter. She joins the 29.1 million single female heads of household in 1984.[26] Child care in the United States is provided through a mix of services of public and private agencies. There are some government funded programs and some private agencies that receive public funds. There is a definite lack of quality child care in this country, basically because of the ideological conflict over the role of women. The majority of working women in the United States are dependent on relatives, friends, or neighbors to provide day care for their young children.[27] President Nixon vetoed child-care legislation in 1971 because of its "family-weakening" implications; yet in the same year, he signed new welfare rules with Work Incentives that required all women to register for work. The reality of the 1980s is that mothers have to work and need better child care facilities. The existent day care facilities are really geared to the low-income mother and thus limit the eligibility for any middle-income parent. The costs of private day care often are prohibitive. In the case of mothers who are victims of violence, they have no choice but to work and to demand safe child care. The ambivalence of the government's public policies on this issue only damages future generations.

The ongoing *reality*, not the ideological conflict over the role of the mother of young children should be the deciding factor. There are more divorces and more violence in the American home so that child care for younger children is imperative. The median weekly wage for the female single parent household was $267 in 1984.[28] This will not support a family and provide child care and necessary medical services. This is why most mothers have to use a hit or miss arrangement with neighbors and relatives. This is the Catch-23 referred to in an article in the *Social Work Journal*.[29] Society continues to locate woman's place as in the home; yet when the home breaks up, as often happens in violent situations, the woman is expected to go to work to support her children. The job market offers her few opportunities and low pay. Public day care is almost nonexistent. But on low public assistance, food stamps, and Medicaid, her family *cannot* survive. The AFDC program allows no extra room for children's emergencies, no Christmas presents, no transportation to see relatives and nothing for the teenagers' need to be equal to their peers. Usually utility bills are neglected so that children's needs are met and a mother may lose her housing, her heat, electricity, or water. *This economic reality is the reason so many women and children remain trapped in violent home situations in this prosperous country.*

The conclusions to be drawn from this dilemma faced by all women seeking to support their families is the need for a drastic change in governmental policy decisions. There has been debate since the early 1970s on the need for welfare reform. One possible solution would be an elimination of the bureaucracy of present welfare programs; a family assistance payment plan that is not *punitive*; and that would guarantee a decent living standard to *anyone* below a certain income level. The second change necessary in government policy to produce a mentally and physically healthy younger generation in the United States would be more funding and other forms of government support for day-care services. Since women are not always able to stay home with young children, it is essential for their emotional well-being while at work, and their children's good health, that quality day-care facilities be available at affordable rates. Child-care facilities could be funded as an earlier function of the educational system. Head Start programs are being encouraged again in the 1980s.

Thus the basic policies that need to be changed are in the economic structure. It is critical when evaluating the victims of family violence to understand the impact of the economic factor on the future lives of these victims. Economic discrimination against women and children who refuse to depend on males for their support is encoded in the law. Public assistance programs continue punitive in their policies toward single-parent families; and 90 percent of these families are headed by females.

The basic economic change should be in better job opportunities and higher wages for women. In the meantime, public assistance policies should be turned around to grant mothers and their children the health-enriched opportunities that are the entitlement of all the citizens of this country.

NOTES

1. U. S. Department of Labor *Handbook of labor statistics*, Bureau of Labor Statistics. June 1985, Bulletin #2217.
2. Pogrebin, L. C. *Getting yours: How to make the system work for the working woman.* New York: David McKay, 1975.

3. Nochlin, L. Why are there no great women artists. In V. Cromick, & B. Moran. (Eds.), *Women in sexist society: Studies in power and powerlessness.* New York: Basic Books, 1971.

4. Hunter College Women's Studies Collective Women's Realities, *Women's choices.* New York: Oxford University Press, 1983.

5. Gold, D. B. Women and voluntarism. In *Women in sexist society,* op. cit., p. 541.

6. Adams, M. The compassion trip. In *Women in sexist society,* p. 556.

7. Loeser, H. *Women, work, and volunteering.* Boston: Beacon Press, 1974, p. 31.

8. Foner, P. S. *Women and the American Labor Movement: From World War I to the present.* New York: Free Press, 1980.

9. Ibid.

10. U. S. Department of Labor, op cit.

11. Knapman, S. K. Sex discrimination in family agencies. *Social Work.* November 1977, New York: National Association of Social Workers.

12. Bergmann, B. Comparable worth for professors. In *Academe,* American Association of University Professors July–August 1985, p. 8.

13. Backhouse, C. & Cohen, L. *Sexual harassment on the job.* Englewood Cliffs, NJ: Prentice Hall, 1981.

14. Ibid., p. 34.

15. Ibid., p. 35.

16. Farley, L. *Sexual shakedown: Sexual harassment of women on the job.* New York: McGraw Hill, 1978.

17. Kanter, R. M. *Men and women of the corporation.* New York: Basic Books, 1977. Chapter 4.

18. Harragan, B. L. *Games mother never taught you: Corporate gamesmanship for women.* New York: Rawson Associates, 1977, p. 10.

19. Ibid., Chapters 2, 3.

20. Lever, J. Sex differences in games children play. *Social Problems 23* (1976), pp. 478–487.

21. United States Commission for UNESCO. *Report on Women in America.* Department of State Publications, November 1977.

22. Norman, E., & Mancuso, A. *Women's issues and social work practice.* Itasco, Illinois: F. E. Peacock, 1980.

23. U. S. Social Security Administration Office of Research and Statistics, Washington, D.C. May 1984 Bulletin.

24. Ibid.
25. Gilbert, N., & Specht, H. *The emergence of social welfare and social work*. In M. Wolins, Societal function of social welfare. Itasca, Illinois: F. E. Peacock. 1975, p. 118.
26. U. S. Department of Labor, op. cit., p. 117.
27. Dinerman, M. Catch 23, Women, work and welfare, *Social Work*, National Association of Social Workers, New York. November 1977, p. 474.
28. U. S. Department of Labor Statistics, op. cit., p. 92.
29. Dinerman, M. op. cit., p. 476.

Chapter 3

THE LEGAL SYSTEM FOR VICTIMS OF FAMILY VIOLENCE

Edward Mullarkey

Wives who have been battered, women who have been raped, and children who have been abused all need the support of the legal institutions in this country. Many of them fail to seek legal sanctions against their offenders because of fear or ignorance of the law. It is fundamental that both the victims of violence and social workers have an understanding of how a case of violence is processed by the District Attorney, the police, and the entire legal system. Many states are concluding that arrest and prosecution of family members who commit violent acts are the best solution. The victim is relieved of guilt and the family has a breathing period in which to reorganize and to use various helping professionals, such as social workers and lawyers, to best plan their future.

The interaction between the prosecutor and social worker in a case of domestic violence is an association which presents enormous potential for mutual benefit. However, the different duties, goals, and priorities of each pose serious threats to reaching the results sought. The description which follows of the role of the prosecutor is generally accurate throughout the United States, although many local variations exist. Recent and long-overdue strides made in victim rights and victim advocacy are as yet not universally available.

THE CRIMINAL JUSTICE SYSTEM

In this country the criminal justice system is based on a complex compound of federal and state constitutions, legislation, and court decisions. In many states it has the authority to execute persons convicted of crime in general, and domestic assault in particular. These sentences are the final product of the system. Whether they produce the desired results is open to much speculation and study. But, with the exception of conditions placed on defendants for their release before a trial is held or a sentence put into effect, these are the only tools the system has to control defendants who are competent to stand trial and were sane at the time of the offense.

As an institution of social control, the criminal justice system is too full of delay and too lacking in certainty. Once an arrest is made, the momentum in the legal system shifts to the defense. Motions attacking the jurisdiction of the court, the legality of the arrest, and the validity of a search or confession are only a few of many standard defense motions to which the prosecution must respond. Court dockets are too crowded and the pressure of business too often pushes domestic cases to the bottom of the list. Plea bargaining is the norm and some lawyers view a jury trial as a breakdown in the system. Incarcerated defendants are tried first even if their arrests occurred after that of another defendant who made bond. The longer the delay in a domestic case, the less likely it is that a witness will want to appear, or will retain accurate recollections of the events when questioned. The system is rooted in the paramount value of individual rights which guard against a potentially oppressive sovereign. Who designed this? Nobody did.

The last architect of the American criminal justice system was a Frenchman who ruled England from 1154 to 1189. He put into practice reforms instituted by his grandfather and began some of his own. In order to establish control over his realm and raise revenue, he created a new system of royal justice with a professional cadre of itinerant judges. The right to trial by jury became an alternative to a trial by combat, ordeal, or compurgation (in which only the accused's character was an issue, not the facts). Offenses against a person or a person's property began to be viewed as offenses against the king's peace. Over the centuries the victim lost the necessity, and then the right, to be the complaining party in a criminal case.[1] These legacies of Henry II are still controlling principles of the American criminal justice system. The sovereign, the people, is the complainant in all criminal cases. The other party is the defendant. There is no third party.[2]

Brought to the Colonies and refined by the American experience, the English common law retained its inherent capacity to change by judicial decision. The most important innovation is the Bill of Rights, which gives persons suspected or accused of crime minimum rights throughout this country. States may not infringe upon these guarantees but may grant additional rights. This written set of guarantees to defendants is not matched by any similar provision for victims.

All three branches of government meet in court. The legislative branch supplies the funding and the substantive criminal statutes. The judicial branch interprets these statutes, determines procedure and tests the actions of law enforcement officials against the standards set forth in the procedures, statutes, and Bill of Rights. When added to the annual or semiannual legislative changes in statutes, the continuous stream of judicial decisions keeps the system in a constant state of flux. Usually at the option of the defendant, a judge may also act as the trier of fact, innocence, or guilt, in a criminal case. The executive branch is represented by the prosecutor.

Whether elected or appointed, the prosecutor represents the state in all criminal matters. The prosecutor does not represent the victim or the police. Except for investigators who have the power of arrest and work directly for the prosecutor, the prosecutor has no direct control over the police. All prosecutors are sworn to uphold the Constitution, statutes, and code of professional responsibility of their respective jurisdictions.

Within this structure, prosecutors are given vast authority and discretion in the initiation and disposition of criminal cases. Warrantless arrests made by police for crimes committed in their presence or upon speedy information do not become criminal cases until they are filed by the prosecutor with the court. Arrest warrants are either not issued without the prosecutor's approval, or the charges they contain are not proceeded with if the prosecutor declines to prosecute.

In addition to the charging function, the prosecutor represents the state's case in court. The prosecutor makes and argues motions for the state and responds to those made by the defense. Through witnesses for the state, the prosecutor presents evidence to the trier of fact—either a judge or a jury. Prosecutors also occasionally bring appeals of court decisions unfavorable to the state, but they are more likely to be responding to appeals brought by the defense after conviction. Over 90 percent of criminal cases are disposed of without trial. In plea negotiation the prosecutor reduces a charge and/or limits potential sentencing in return for a plea of guilty.

The prosecutor's pivotal role in the criminal justice system can help accomplish a social worker's goals in a particular case. Even though a prosecutor's actions are, for the most part, reviewable by the courts and limited by the law, the prosecutor can overturn a police refusal to arrest if probable cause exists. A prosecutor influences the conditions under which a defendant is released from custody. Psychiatric and substance-abuse screening and treatment can be ordered in addition to, or in lieu of, cash or surety bonds. Dispositions of cases frequently include treatment requirements and provisions limiting or prohibiting contact with victims. Criminal and administrative search warrants open the most guarded locations. While custody and restraining orders are in the civil courts and generally beyond the prosecutor's jurisdiction, violation of such orders is increasingly becoming a crime.

THE ROLE OF THE SOCIAL WORKER IN THE LEGAL SYSTEM

Whether attached directly to some agency within the criminal justice system or, as is more typical, working for an outside agency, a social worker can have significant impact. Most prosecutors need more staff in their offices. Too often that lack leads to less time spent communicating with victims. The priority assigned to domestic violence cases, especially spouse battering, is sometimes low because of a misunderstanding of its importance or an impression that a criminal proceeding is not going to produce any results. All prosecutors need more facts, both those which can be proved in court and those which provide an understanding of the background to the case.

In five areas, social workers can provide invaluable aid to the prosecutor and the victim.

1. It is frightening how little information is provided to the prosecutor in the most commonly brought type of domestic violence case, spousal battering. Unless hospital admission occurs or a weapon is involved, the complete investigation is handled by an overworked patrolman as the part of one shift. The report to the prosecutor will contain the time and place of the assault, the officer's observations of the victim's injuries, the names of witnesses, the identity of the defendant, and a summary of the statements made by each. The prosecutor will also receive a copy of the defendant's record of criminal convictions containing no notations of who the victims of those crimes were. *Providing more information* is the first area in which the social worker can be helpful.

2. Fortunately there is a decreasing need for the second type of help a social worker can provide, *education*. Law school is not a particularly sensitizing experience. Dealing constantly with the behavior recorded in prosecutors' files promotes further despair about the human condition. All too often, conviction rates become a substitute for justice. Victims' concerns become subordinated in the crush of business. Appropriate and timely reminders of the society beyond the courthouse are sometimes needed.

3. The most important service which a social worker can provide to a prosecutor is to *transfer trust*. Victims and other witnesses of domestic violence are usually more frightened and bewildered than those in most other types of cases. They are more often threatened and influenced by defendants and other members of the family. What appears to be victory for the prosecutor—conviction and incarceration of the defendant—often looms as a future filled with mixed relief and guilt for the victim. Prosecutors seldom have the hours to devote to securing the trust necessary to transform a victim into an effective witness who will not be more harmed than helped by the court system. Convincing the victim to confide in and trust the prosecutor is not an easy task, but must be

accomplished by the social worker if cases are to be brought to successful conclusions.

4. Acting as an *advocate* for the victim during all stages of a criminal case is the fourth function a social worker can perform. Victims need an experienced guide to get them through the maze of the criminal justice system. No law prevents a social worker from stating the victim's side to the prosecutor, even before an arrest is made. Nor does anything prohibit such communication while a case is pending at the trial or appellate stage.

Over the past several years, victims or their advocates have been gaining the right to speak at court or board hearings. The trend toward allowing victims or their representatives to speak at important junctures in the process has opened new opportunities in victim advocacy. Many jurisdictions permit the victim or the victim advocate to address the judge at sentencing. Some states are allowing and inviting such presentations at bond and parole board hearings. Being a supportive companion to a victim when the time has come to testify does more than those who have never seen a witness break down on the stand could imagine. This support is essential for the victim who is reliving the violent traumatic experience.

5. Except for the laws governing a case, evidence is the most important factor in any criminal proceeding. Gathering *evidence* is the job of the police. When tangible evidence such as clothing, photographs, or documents come into the possession of a social worker, they should be turned in to the police immediately. A note should be made of the officer's name and badge number, and a receipt obtained if possible. Meticulous records are necessary to prove a chain of custody prior to introducing most real, physical, evidence in court.

Absent a court order, neither social workers nor victims are required to speak to defendants, their attorneys, or their investigators outside the courtroom. Consult the prosecutor for any variations in local rules. Anything said to a social worker by a witness may become testimonial evidence. Careful notes should be kept. A social worker may be allowed to testify to what the victim said as a part of the state's proof against a defendant or a cross-examination by the defendant's attorney. Every note and report prepared by a social worker is potentially discoverable by the defendant. No shield law can, or will, ever provide a guarantee. The constitutional guarantee to confront accusers provided by the Sixth Amendment can be interpreted by any competent court to override any privacy statute or shield law. (See *State v. Sheppard*) in Appendix for a discussion of the Sixth Amendment on a similar issue.) The prosecutor can help social workers to learn how to present evidence in factual, legal manner.

When testifying in court, a social worker should be professional, not partisan. Questions should be answered directly and fully. Unclear questions will be clarified upon request. A social worker should find the time to go over proposed questions with the prosecutor before testifying. This is standard procedure, not something to be embarrassed about when defense counsel mentions it in cross-examination.

Expert testimony involves drawing conclusions based on facts refined through education and experience. Traditionally confined within strict limits as to qualifications, expert testimony has been quietly expanding. The more professional education and clinical practice a social worker has, the more likely it is that his/her opinions will be admitted into evidence. Being able to explain a victim's passive and dependent behavior as the result of child abuse syndrome is one type of opinion testimony which is being presently admitted in many courts. As yet, the expansion into this area has been slowly accumulating at the trial level of the court system.

ISSUES

Not only victims have social workers. Those social workers who have defendants as clients have an equal need to establish a good working relationship with the prosecutor. The cold facts contained in most police reports are inadequate to guide the prosecutor to the best result to seek in many cases of domestic violence. An informed recommendation from a trusted social worker has often made the difference. Even in those cases in which the crime(s) of the defendant are so terrible or so chronic as to mandate incarceration, the recommendations of a defendant's social worker can influence the length of the incarceration and the terms of the probation which may follow. Domestic violence comprises a long list of physical acts of striking, restraining, molesting, raping, torturing, and murdering. Domestic violence is an enormous social problem. It is a tort at civil law. It is man's all too frequent inhumanity directed against those least able to protect themselves. It is also a crime; and a crime is a crime is a crime.

A crime is an act which society has determined may result in incarceration. For the purposes of determining if a crime has been committed and who committed it, an incredibly intricate structure of laws and institutions has been created. While the victims of crime should have the right to be heard at many points in the criminal justice system, they should not have the right to determine punishment. The victim bears no responsibility for the act which brought the defendant to face justice. The defendant is charged with violating society's rules. Society through the entity of the state formally complains.

The determination of punishment by the victim is often described incorrectly as a system of private vengeance. In cases of domestic violence the victim more often seeks mercy for the defendant than vengeance or justice. Too much pressure is already put on the victim by the system, the family, and the defendant. This is particularly true when a child is held responsible for sending the wage earner away. Often pressured by the rest of the family, frightened by the criminal justice system, and screened by youth from a wider view of the world, the child victim refuses to proceed. Too often the victim is the one emotionally and physically excluded from the home. What is the proper function of the social worker?

The trend toward treating the whole family creates problems as yet unsolved for the criminal justice system. The social worker is not an agent of the prosecutor. Just as discussions with the victim may become the subject of questioning in court, so may the social worker's discussions with a defendant. Counseling which includes continued contact between the child victim and the molester seriously violates the traditional separation sought in criminal cases. It also appears to place an impossible burden on the victim in an attempt to accomplish seldom achieved goals.

Some families cannot be saved. Domestic violence by the defendant has destroyed them. The victims should be convinced that they are not responsible for their own victimization. The social worker needs to make difficult choices if successful relationships of mutual trust with their clients and with prosecutors are to be maintained.

CONCLUSIONS AND RECOMMENDATIONS

Professional associations, victims' rights groups, and individual lobbying have brought great advances in recent years. The modest proposals that follow are basically without cost to the taxpayer. Some already exist in certain jurisdictions. The introduction of videotaped or other out-of-court testimony has opened new possibilities in the prosecution of child abuse cases. The case of *State v. Sheppard* is reprinted in the Appendix because it contains an excellent discussion of the balancing which courts must do between the rights of defendants and the gains which are sought for victims. Many states are enacting statutes considering legislation similar to this decision. It is important to protect children when they have to be witnesses. Victims and their advocates should get the opportunity to speak to the person(s) making the decisions at each critical stage of the criminal justice system from the first responding police officer to the pardon board.

A fee collected from every defendant found guilty of a crime should go to a victim's compensation fund. This fund should be used to defray costs for victims' medical expenses including counseling. Funds should also be dispensed to help with living expenses if injury to the victim or incarceration of the defendant causes economic distress. Too many victims and parents endure the violence to maintain the income provided by the defendant. Violations of conditions of release imposed by courts in addition to or in lieu of bond should be felonies. This would allow police to make arrests upon the complaint of the victim without waiting for the cumbersome steps necessary to have the bond revoked. Finally, the expertise possessed by many social workers should receive formal recognition by accepting into evidence their expert opinions concerning the syndromes displayed by their clients.

NOTES

1. Maitland, F. W. *The constitutional history of England.* Cambridge, England: University Press, 1965.
2. Lunt, W. E. *History of England.* 4th ed., New York: Harper & Row, 1957, pp. 106–120.

Chapter 4

A SOCIAL WORKER'S RESPONSE

Margaret Martin

Social workers are increasingly playing important roles within the criminal justice system, especially in regard to the administration of justice for victims of family violence. The legal system in the United States based upon English Common Law has historically viewed both women and children as the property of the male head of household. It is within this context that social workers intervene both to assist victims in achieving their goals within the system and advocating for the rights of those groups which have been ignored or violated in the criminal justice system as a whole.

The American criminal justice system is a complex of interlocking and sometimes contradictory organizations, entities, laws, decisions, and procedures which, because of its strict boundaries between units and varying goals, has often been classified as a "non-system." As an institution of social control bounded by certain rights and responsibilities it operates in an adversarial style. The institution itself is a reflection of societal values and, as such, is dynamic and evolving. Social workers, then, can play key roles in interpreting changing American values and promoting those consistent with a social work value base, including human dignity, equality, and freedom.

A Victim's View

Numerous graphic accounts have been written about the insensitivity and lack of effectiveness of the criminal justice system in regard to victims of family violence. Countless stories are untold. As illustration of this phenomenon, imagine a woman who has endured numerous beatings at the hands of her spouse, and who, after being beaten again, in desperation and in need of immediate assistance, calls the police. In some jurisdictions police may not respond because of the "domestic" nature of the crime; in many more, a non-arrest procedure mandates that the police "cool off" the situation, perhaps warn the offender, and refer the parties for social service help.

Even at this initial point of entry into the system, the victim is discouraged from pursuing the protection that is her constitutional right. Police may continue to ignore requests for substantial help or arrest because of the lack of successful prosecution of these cases, frustration with the parties, an apparent lack of evidence, or other reasons. If a beating is particularly brutal or the police are prepared to deal adequately with the problem, an arrest may be made. The accused will likely not be removed from the home, but arraigned and free pending his appearance at a later court date. During this time he may continue to harass the victim or dissuade her from cooperating with the prosecution.

Prosecutors may at this juncture refuse to prosecute such cases or refuse to issue warrants for arrest requested by police or victims. In 1966 in Washington, D.C., about 7,500 women requested prosecutors to issue warrants for their husbands' arrest. Less than 200 such warrants were issued.[1] The battered woman may find the prosecutor unwilling to press for prosecution because of the relationship of the parties, fear that she will not cooperate, or the lack of a prior criminal record of the accused. Should prosecution be attempted, judges may refuse to convict and encourage the parties to mediate or solve the dispute. A successful first conviction of assault on a spouse usually involves no incarceration of the offender, and usually represents only one of dozens of previously committed assaults against her. Even in such "successful" outcomes, victims are left exhausted, fearful, and guilty.

Social Work and the Criminal Justice System

Social Work as a profession operates at the intersection of the person and the environment and affects change within both the individual and the systems with which he or she interacts. The social worker assists the victim in understanding the boundaries of the system, the limits of individual power and control, the roles played by various actors, and the like. Similarly, workers facilitate understanding of the needs of victims and promote the rights of victims and witnesses within the existing framework.

As a public system, the criminal justice system must be both accessible and accountable. Social workers play vital roles in assuring that the system is both. As advocates for change, social workers have played leading roles throughout the country in promoting legislation that provides increased protection for victims of family violence and greater ability to meet their needs as victims within the system. The passage of emergency orders of protection, marital rape legislation, admissibility of videotaped testimony of children, mandatory police training in family violence, and other such enacted laws are examples of the significant impact that social workers can have in promoting the accountability of the police and courts.

The Role of the Social Worker in the Legal System

Social workers play a variety of roles in regard to each component of the legal system, including police, prosecutor, and judge. The roles they play, however, may be conflicting, may be viewed differently by various actors, and may promote conflict with social work values and ethical stands. Edward Mullarkey describes the various roles played by social workers as: 1) information provider; 2) social watchdog and educator; 3) facilitator of trust; 4) advocate; and 5) expert witness.

Prior to reviewing each of these roles, it is imperative to discuss the goal of social work intervention. The client's goal and, for the purpose of this discussion, the victim's goal, must be clearly identified and understood. Regardless of the practice setting, whether within the criminal justice system or out, the client's goals must take precedence to other system or social goals (except in cases of physical harm or illegal activity). It is from our understanding of the collective goals of victims as a group and specifically the victims of family violence, that we promote system wide change in their treatment.

It is imperative that a social worker assist the client in identifying and articulating realistic goals for the legal process. Certainly many battered women are discouraged and distrustful of a criminal justice system that has either been ineffectual in protecting her from harm and/or clearly discriminatory in its practices of protecting citizens.

The Tracey Thurman suit against the Torrington, Connecticut Police Department, in which the Department was found guilty of violating the civil rights of battered women, is an example of such unconstitutional practice. While as social workers we may promote the involvement of the criminal justice system in crimes that occur within families, both to protect the individuals and to promote greater justice for all, this is a bias which should clearly be stated to clients. Studies evaluating the level of satisfaction of victims of non-stranger violence with the court outcome have shown that satisfaction levels were not correlated with the actual disposition of the case but with the victim's perception that the physical abuse had stopped and/or that the defendant received the appropriate punishment or treatment.[2] In that more than half of these victims were dissatisfied, and in recognizing the significant expenditure of resources to pursue action within the criminal justice setting, it is important that workers inform clients about the process and possible outcomes.

In working with victims, both protection from continued harm and an appropriate outcome of either punishment or treatment are generally identified as goals. Other goals often articulated are the need for public affirmation of the offender's guilt; a sense of personal vindication; retribution; or a regained sense of control. In all areas it is important to assist the client in understanding the risks in pursuing such goals; the chances of success; her role as both a victim and a State's witness in the State's case against the perpetrator; and her actual minimal control over the outcome of the case.

Because of a variety of factors within the criminal justice system, not the least of which may be a discriminatory attitude toward women and children victims of family violence, it is also important to assist the client in establishing and achieving goals outside the system. For both child and adult victims of family violence, a regained sense of personal control is essential. It is important, then, that the social worker not sabotage the client's efforts to succeed by holding the successful outcome of the court process as a measure of the client's abilities or worth, but rather help the client disengage her sense of personal worth or power from the outcome of the court process.

THE SOCIAL WORKER AS COMMUNICATOR

A vital role that social workers play in assisting their clients is that of communicator. Social workers can be a vehicle for information from the victim to the police or prosecutor or from these parties to the victim. Often the social worker can provide information that is enhanced with empathy and can provide the time to assist the victim in comprehending the information and integrating this with her/his goals and values. The worker should continually educate her/himself about the system and clearly acknowledge personal limitations to all parties. The worker must tread a fine line between communicating and assisting while purposely avoiding advice giving or providing legal information which are the purview of attorneys.

A variety of pitfalls, however, may be encountered in this role. One is the common expectation placed upon the worker outside the system to act as an agent of the prosecutor or police in defending or apologizing for the system. More commonly, the worker is asked to play the essential role of informing the victim of court dates and procedures. While of importance, it may remove the pressure for the office to provide this information uniformly for all victims and not only for those with advocates. Another major area of concern is that of confidentiality. The worker must clearly indicate to the victim that their communication is confidential. Release of information to any criminal justice personnel should be only with the written consent of the client, and the police and prosecutor should be informed of the social worker's obligations in this area. The worker may often be expected to release all information as an aid to police investigation or prosecution.[3]

THE SOCIAL WORKER AS EDUCATOR

The NASW Code of Ethics states that social workers ". . . should advocate changes in policy and legislation to improve social conditions and to promote social justice."[4] In working with victims of family violence, the social worker has a dual responsibility to be educated by system actors, such as police, prosecutors, and judges, as well as to inform and remind them of their obligations to ensure equality of access, the role of sex-role stereotyping, the social and emotional effects of discrimination upon victims, the dynamics of victimization and other relevant social and psychological facts. Social workers also can provide information about relevant research, policies, and activities that enhance the position of victims within the criminal justice system.

THE SOCIAL WORKER AS FACILITATOR OF TRUST

Social workers can assist in the development of trust between prosecutor and victim, an element essential to successful prosecution of family violence cases. Should the victim indicate that prosecution is a goal, then providing the most accurate and complete review of the facts and circumstances surrounding the crime is critical to the ability to prosecute. Victims should be aware of the goal of the system, to "successfully" achieve a guilty verdict, and fully understand their role as witnesses for the State against the defendant. The police and prosecutor should clearly state the limits of their roles, or the social worker should identify them, in order to assure commonality of expectations. If the battered woman, for instance, does not believe that the prosecutor is empowered to intervene with her abusing husband, or wishes to actively seek a conviction, then she will have little incentive to disclose intimidation or threat by the defendant.

The system actors must, in turn, regard family violence as serious crime and treat victims with dignity and respect in order to receive their trust. The social worker must also work to improve policies and procedures that enhance the position of victims within the justice system in order to facilitate continued and deserving trust.

THE SOCIAL WORKER AS ADVOCATE

An increasingly accepted role of social workers is that of client advocate. Within the criminal justice system the social worker must learn the complexities of the variety of system components: law enforcement, prosecution, corrections, etc., and continually keep the client's goals in focus. As the role of advocate becomes accepted within the criminal justice system, it is imperative that social workers act to empower clients to act in their own behalf whenever possible. This will not only provide the victim with valuable life skills, but will work to assure that individuals continue to be respected and recognized within the criminal justice system without an intermediary.

As an advocate for victims of family violence, the social worker acts to interpret the system to the client; acts as a consultant to the client in helping her reach her goals; acts to empower the client to develop skills useful in other aspects of life; and works to promote the interests of victims as a group. The worker, with the client's permission, may also act as an agent for the victim in promoting her interests with key system actors. Social work tasks may vary from persuading police to arrest, to recommending a particular sentence based upon the victim's preference; from pressuring court personnel to secure a private and safe waiting area for victims, to notifying a probation officer of a violation of a condition of parole.

Workers who act advocates, but also who provide support and assistance, have the difficult task of helping victims to resolve the emotional and physical consequences of their victimization, while maintaining accurate and vivid recollection of the crime in order to successfully prosecute weeks, months, or even a year after the incident.

THE SOCIAL WORKER AS EXPERT WITNESS

The role of social workers as expert witnesses is becoming increasingly legitimized and pursued. Many workers seek the opportunity to provide professional information in court settings to promote understanding about the behavior of victims and offenders. While many social workers welcome the opportunity to provide such information, they resist the notion of releasing under court order information which they view as confidential. In spite of efforts to protect communication with clients from subpoena, social workers increasingly find it necessary to surrender files and client information to civil and criminal proceedings.

SOCIAL WORK ISSUES IN FAMILY VIOLENCE

Social work practice with victims of domestic violence produces a variety of ethical and practice dilemmas. Those cited by Edward Mullarkey, that of confidential communication and the emphasis on family treatment in child abuse cases are but two. Workers must comprehend the complexity of the issues addressed and the significance of the deprivation of freedom which is the consequence of many criminal proceedings.

Issues to be explored include:

An understanding of racial and ethnic discrimination throughout the criminal justice system. Minorities are overrepresented in arrest, prosecution, conviction, and sentencing. They are more likely to be sentenced to time in prison and less likely to receive alternative sentences than whites. As social workers advocating for criminal penalties for perpetrators of family violence, how do we not become complicit in a set of discriminatory practices?

In assisting clients in achieving their goals, we may promote an individual's deprivation of liberty and the assignment of a stigmatizing role. Are these actions contrary to social work values?

The evolving use of mediation and special family courts, while reducing the adversarial approach of the regular court processes, may provide second-class justice for family violence victims or promote a negotiated resolution which is the result of unequal power and therefore an unfair resolution.

What is the social worker's responsibility to warn a party when a victim discusses revenge?

In promoting the best interests of victims individually and as a group, a social worker has responsibility to promote and assure the civil liberties of all citizens. Social workers have an obligation not to support practices which deprive individuals of their civil liberties, such as working with victims or criminal justice agents to entrap defendants.

CONCLUSION

Social workers can play important roles in helping family violence victims achieve their goals in the criminal justice system. Whether through individual or system advocacy, the criminal justice system can respond to victims' needs by providing protection from further violence and through correctional efforts or treatment for the offender. The system, however, continues to be a complex web of individuals, procedures, and policies, often with conflicting values, based upon a patriarchal legal system, and reflective of societal discrimination based upon sex, age, class, race, and ethnicity. Numerous studies have documented battered women's discouragement with police intervention and lack of faith in the criminal court's ability to meet their needs.

A National Institute of Justice Report on the criminal court's response to non-stranger violence documented that more than one-half of all victims emerged from the court process with negative feelings about the officials and the process.[5] Other studies have consistently shown that decided response from the criminal justice system, whether arrest of perpetrator, vigorous prosecution, or stern warnings by judges, result in lessened violence in the family. Social work can exercise a critical function in assisting victims in asserting their needs and in changing the system to be more responsive to the violence experienced in families.

NOTES

1. Fields, M. Wife beating: Government intervention policies and practices, *Battered women: Issues of public policy.* A Consultation Sponsored by the U.S. Civil Rights Commission, U.S. Government Printing Office, 1978, p. 249.
2. U.S. Department of Justice, National Institute of Justice, *Non-Stranger violence: The Criminal Court's response.* U.S. Government Printing Office, 1983, p. 94.
3. Curtis, P. A., & Lutkus, A. M., Client confidentiality in police social work settings, *Social Work,* 1985, *30*(4).
4. NASW, The National Association of Social Workers, *Code of Ethics,* 1975.
5. U.S. Department of Justice, ibid., 94.

Chapter 5

BATTERED WOMEN

Margaret Martin

That the most serious physical injury that a woman is likely to experience in this society is from the man to whom she is, or has been married, is a frightening and shocking reality. Until the 1970s the myth that the family provided protection and support to its members prevailed. Yet the public awareness of the facts— that 1.8 million women are beaten annually in the United States[1]— provides an apparent contradiction to all that we have believed about human relationships. While most persons recognized that conflict existed within marital relationships, and some realized inherent problems in the institution of marriage, few expected the pervasiveness or seriousness of the violence that we have learned characterize the relationships of women and men in family settings.

Why can half of all married women expect to experience a violent episode in her relationship?[2] Why are at least one-quarter of all women murdered in this country killed by men with whom they are, or have been, in an intimate relationship?[3] Why is one woman beaten by her husband every 18 seconds in the United States?[4] The search for answers continues to generate apparent dichotomies: the juxtaposition of love with violence, and of protection with injury; remaining in a relationship that may include violence, rather than fleeing; or the commission of heinous crimes by an apparently gentle man. In asking the question *why* we pursue a philosophical quest. But to learn more about the phenomenon of this form of violence against women, we must ask the question, how does this violence occur?

Clearly, the phenomenon of woman-battering exists within a context of generalized violence against women in this society. Its most extreme form, the murder of an intimate, is the most dangerous. It has its roots in the historical oppression of women by men; is condoned by our cultural mores and values; and is legitimized within legal and religious institutions. The study of battered women must be a political study that examines the control exercised by men over women with whom they are in relationship. For it is not simply a study of aggression or of a dysfunctional family system.

While different from other forms of violence against women, such as rape and pornography, it does share common elements in commission and consequence. While the larger cultural and historical perspectives are necessary to our understanding of the problem and our ability to institute change, battering has enormous psychological consequences and social implications which also must be explored. Given social work's previous inattention to the problem, it must now assure through its practitioners' skills and values that it is part of the solution to this major social problem.

WOMAN-BATTERING IN HISTORICAL PERSPECTIVE

Contemporary literature, journalistic accounts, and legal history have recorded the nature of wife-battering in Western culture. (I will purposely use the term wife-battering interchangeably with woman-battering, since most historical accounts record violence within the spectrum of this legitimized relationship. Most research documents that violence against women in cohabiting relationships is similar to that against wives.) From the depiction of subjugated women on Roman vases to the archetype of the working-class hero, Ralph Cramden, who persistently threatens to punch his wife Alice "to the moon," in a popular 1950s television series, the media depict the array of "appropriate" violent behaviors for men to engage in. Whatever our cultural context, we have been socialized to the acceptance of violence against women in their relationships. From Charles Perrault's depictions in *Mother Goose* to the award of the Nobel Peace Prize to Prime Minister Sato of Japan, previously accused of wife-battering, violence against women intimates has not been considered a social problem but rather a fact of life.

Del Martin, Dobash and Dobash, Terry Davidson, and other authors provide comprehensive accounts of battering in history. Their descriptions detail the foundation and framework for the establishment of a patriarchal order which is enforced by the use of violence. The Roman order was based upon the family unit as the major social grouping. Only the upper or patrician classes, however, were afforded the distinction of legitimized marriage, for they alone owned property that was to be controlled and inherited. Women were purchased as brides and treated as additions to the husband's property. The grouping, known as *familia*, included a man, with his wife, children, and slaves, over whom the husband had the right of life and death. During this period the wife's status was closely akin to that of a slave. She was responsible for bearing and raising the husband's children, and subjected to violent beatings or death if she acted contrary to his wishes or to the social code of the time.

Many of the Roman social customs regarding women were carried through the Middle Ages. The practice of monogamy and legitimized marriage were more widespread due to the stronger influence of Christianity. During this period also, the subordination of women to men was closely enforced. Men were encouraged to chastise their wives, and to beat or even kill them should infidelity be suspected. Even some of the minor gains made by women in personal liberty during this period were erased during later centuries as the social order throughout western Europe and the colonial New World became more rigid and stratified.

Throughout recorded Western history we note that the hierarchical structure of society was maintained through social institutions, such as law, and a supportive ideology. Even until the twentieth century, vestiges of the legal view of women as property, rather than full human beings, remained. Consequently, as law developed during these periods, it provided permission to husbands for the brutal beatings or even murder of their wives.

English common law, upon which law in the United States is based, suggested limits such as "rule of thumb," to the physical "chastisement" of wives, based upon the seriousness of the offense. But murder for infidelity and the legal system's refusal to intervene in family disputes persisted even through the twentieth century.

Although the institutions of marriage and the law provided the social framework to maintain the patriarchal order, belief and value systems solidified the control men exercised over women and assured that women internalized this patriarchal system. The Judeo-Christian ethic remanded women to the authority of their husbands, instructed husbands to physically chastise their wives, and legitimized the subordinate position of women in marriage.[5] Another element which further assisted in the acceptance of the right of male superiority and the dependence of women was the emergence in the eighteenth century of the notion of romantic love. Now that the practices of bride capture and bride purchase became irrelevant within the economic system, women still perceived no control of their choices through the notion that emotional surrender to a greater, controlling force (love), was the preferred basis upon which marriage partnerships should be arranged.

Yet historians' role in describing battering ends, or begins, with the emergence of recorded history. Anthropologists then must assist in our understanding if such brutality toward women by intimates existed prior to this time. Although controversy exists within the anthropological discipline, some anthropologists see the hunting and gathering period of human development characterized by egalitarian tribal units, limited pairing, and a matriarchal organization. Evelyn Reed sees the emergence of the patriarchal family unit as the result of collective forces beginning with the development of agriculture, which broke down the tribal structure and created surplus property. She and others assert that the desire to monopolize property ownership and to transit it through patriarchal lines brought the institution of monogamous marriage and the oppression of women. Although she does not speculate on the use of violence in arranging or maintaining monogamous relationships, other authors allude to its use in the practice of "bride stealing" or "bride capture."

Another explanation for the development of monogamous family units is offered by Susan Brownmiller who states: "Female fear of an open season of rape and not a natural inclination toward monogamy, motherhood, or love, was probably the single causative factor in the original subjugation of women by man, the most important key to her historic dependence, her domination by protective mating.[6] As we understand now, "protective mating" may offer a woman no protection from stranger rape yet increase the possibility of violence, including marital rape, from her chosen partner.

THE PRESENT PROBLEM

It has only been 100 years since Massachusetts became the first state in the United States to legally repudiate "wife-battering." In 1871 it was declared that the "privilege, ancient though it be, to beat her with a stick, to pull her hair, choke her, spit in her face or kick her about the floor, or to inflict upon her other indignities, is not now acknowledged by our law."[7] Slowly other states followed in outlawing battering as women began to be accorded some human rights. Yet although all states now outlaw assault, if the parties are in a relationship, it is unlikely that the laws will be enforced. It has only been since the mid-1970s that services have been provided to women who are beaten in their homes, that we have begun to recognize the seriousness of injury, and the pervasiveness of the problem that has been part of our culture since at least the beginning of written history.

THE DEFINITIONS

A variety of elements comprise the most common definitions of a "battered woman." Generally, social service providers, medical practitioners, sociologists, public policy analysts, and researchers incorporate the following into a working definition:

> *The infliction of physical pain or injury with the intent to cause harm* which may include slaps, punches, biting, and hair pulling, but in frequency or occurrence generally involves more serious assaults including choking, kicking, breaking bones, stabbing, or shooting;

or forcible restraint which may include locking in homes or closets, being tied or handcuffed;

committed by an adult against an adult woman with whom he has or previously had an established relationship, which generally includes physical intimates, whether or not legally married and, less frequently, includes siblings, children, fathers-in-law, and other relatives of adult victims.

Other constructs that are part of accepted definitions include: a frequency of greater than one assault; the threat of physical harm; forcible rape in marriage; or injury without the intent to cause harm. Generally service providers use the least restrictive definitions, researchers, the more narrow and precise. Although most recognize the deleterious effects of emotional abuse, that alone is not considered sufficient for the definition. Emotional abuse is uniformly present with physical abuse[8] and may include constant ridicule and deprecating comments, enforced isolation of the woman from family and friends, accusations of infidelity or mental illness, and threatened suicide or kidnapping of children.

Battering: The Incidence:

Twenty-eight percent of the couples in a probability sample of 2,000 families indicated experiencing a violent incident in their marriage. Accounting for underreporting, the author suggests that the true incidence rate, generalizable to all American couples, is 50 percent to 60 percent.[9]

Data from the National Crime Survey indicates that husbands or ex-husbands are responsible for one-fourth of all assaults against ever-married women and that "Spouse abuse is more likely than other assaults to involve an actual attack rather than a threat. Spouse abuse victims are more likely to be injured, to require medical attention and hospitalization, and to lose time from work. Incidents of spouse abuse were slightly more likely than other assaults to be classified as serious assaults by the NCS Crime Survey."[10]

According to FBI statistics in 1973, one-quarter of all murders occurred within the family, one-half of these were husband-wife killings. Reports from sections of the country which included cohabiting persons or divorced persons were higher. For instance, in 1974, 25 percent of all murders in San Francisco involved legally married or cohabiting mates. When examined in relation to female-only homicide rates, the statistics are even more startling: in California in 1971, one-third of all female homicide victims were murdered by their husbands.[11]

Researchers and authors in the field cite these generalizations about the incidence of battering:

The term spouse abuse distorts the major findings of most researchers and practitioners: overwhelmingly, women are the victims of violence in the home. Some researchers note that 99 percent of the victims are women[12] and that of 450 persons seeking legal remedies from abuse, only two were men.[13] Although some studies, especially those by Steinmetz, Gelles, and Straus point to collaborative violence in the home mutually employed by husbands and wives, some methodological problems give question to these studies. Straus has noted that such findings should not divert attention away from women who are the victims of such assaults because:

Underreporting is greater for violence committed by husbands than by wives.

Husbands have higher rates for the most dangerous and injurious forms of violence.

When violent acts are committed by a husband they are likely to be repeated.

The studies do not show what proportion of acts by wives were in response to blows initiated by husbands.

Previous and subsequent studies show that as being exceedingly high.

A disproportionately large number of attacks by husbands occur when the woman is pregnant.

Women are locked into a marriage to a much greater extent than men.[14]

Other authors note that men use violence as a means of controlling women's behavior; that the studies, indicting the mutuality of violence, lack the context necessary to evaluate whether behaviors were equivalent (as Mildred Pagelow notes, a kick under a bridge table with an open sandal is not equivalent to a kick by a pointed cowboy boot);[15] that male violence against women is accompanied by emotional abuse and abuse becomes more serious over time; and the experience of service providers is that 99 percent of the adult (non-elderly) persons who identify themselves as injured or seeking relief from abuse in the family are women.

The battering of women occurs throughout the socioeconomic spectrum. Battering exists with about the same frequency in rural or urban areas; among blacks, whites, Hispanics, Asians, Native Americans, and other groups; in all religious grouping; among the very poor, middle class, and very wealthy; in young adults and the elderly. Some studies suggest some differences in the form of violence employed, the frequency of violent acts, the willingness to use or the attitude toward the use of violence, and the resources chosen to end violence among different groups. None, however, point to major differences between categories. *What emerges as the most striking characteristic is the basic similarity in the attitude towards and use of violence by all segments of the American population.*

Murder is the most extreme form of violence between intimates and occurs at a startlingly high frequency. Women kill their husbands with about the same frequency that husbands kill their wives, although the motivations and methods appear drastically different. In addition, women who have been the intimates of men, whether as lovers or ex-wives, are much more likely to be murdered by men than the reverse. Overall, women are much likelier than men to be slain in their position as wives or intimates of men than are men in their position of husband.[16]

Murder is usually the culmination of a series of battering incidents that may occur over years, although some over a period of weeks. Men often kill their wives by literally beating them to death; women generally compensate for their size disadvantage by using a weapon. But for women, murder is usually the last desperate act of self-defense against a man who has battered her and stripped her of self-esteem and respect. Studies of persons who murder assert that: Women murderers are motivated by self-defense about seven times more frequently than men;[17] that men who are murdered are more likely to have physically provoked their wives than wives their husbands;[18] and that women who murder usually do so after years of physical abuse by their mates (in one study, 40 percent of the women in the Women's Correctional Center in Chicago who murdered their husbands, common-law husbands, or lovers, committed the crime after years of abuse by their partners).[19]

The Characteristics of Women Who Are Battered and of Men Who Batter

There is clearly enormous diversity in the life-styles, status, personal attributes, and backgrounds of the women who are battered and the men who batter. The difficulty encountered by researchers in discovering significant and generalizable conditions of battered women that distinguish them from non-battered women points to the breadth of the problem. Perhaps it may be easier to study and describe 50 percent of the men who may not engage in violent acts than to isolate characteristics of the batterer. While the classic image of the battered woman is portrayed in many arenas as that of a woman who is immobilized by fear, guilt ridden, isolated, indecisive, and dependent, few have noted her enormous caring for others or her strength in difficult and treacherous situations. The images of these battered women provide a sketch rather than a description of a "typical" battered woman.

1. She is a sixty-year-old woman who left a government career job in her late twenties to marry. Away from all family connections, he has slapped her, attempted to choke her, and has destroyed her possessions throughout the course of the marriage. In attempting to control her behavior, he has signed commitment papers on three occasions to place her temporarily in a state psychiatric hospital. Although protective regulations now exist to prohibit such acts, he continually threatens to "have her committed," and she continually seeks to have her sanity validated.

2. She is a twenty-eight-year-old single mother of two children who met a hardworking man who courted her lovingly. They planned to be married. Offered a better job, he asked her to move out of state. Relocated, he tied her and tortured her. The police charged him with disturbing the peace, but he was never prosecuted. She fled the state, he followed her, found her, and began to harass

her. He broke into her home, abducted her, raped, and attempted to strangle her. Following repeated violations of a restraining order during the court process, he served 3 months in jail.

3.   She is a fifty-eight-year-old mother of two daughters, eighteen and twenty-two. Although she had been slapped and kicked by her husband, she had, on the advice of her minister, chosen to stay with him. Her daughter recently disclosed that the father had sexually assaulted her from the ages of six to thirteen. The mother decided immediately to leave her husband.

Given the widespread nature of the problem, the broad spectrum of behaviors that constitute "battering," and the wide continuum of psychological and sociological characteristics of the abuser and the abused, it is both difficult and often misleading to generalize. Researchers and practitioners have attempted to isolate those characteristics that battered women have in common and those that set them apart from non-battered women, and those of battering men from non-battering men.

Numerous generalizations have been made, some in fact quite contradictory of each other. Feminist researchers have rejected the notion of attempting to isolate differentiating factors. They suggest that it may be chance alone that determines whether a woman will be battered or not, and focus their research efforts on understanding more of the nature of the violence and its implications. Yet, throughout, problems pervade the domestic violence literature. It has been difficult effectively to conduct research in the field because:

Large-scale samples generalizable to the general population are expensive (the emphasis for funding has justifiably been placed on services) and the studies suffer from methodological problems such as:

> - Asking questions of a woman with the perpetrator present, as in the National Crime Survey;
> - Not ascertaining the context in which particular violent acts took place, such as the determination of whether an act was performed in defense or as coercion, and not being able to assess the seriousness of particular acts;
> - Differing or incomplete definitions of violent behaviors;

- The pairing of acts with differing levels of seriousness, such as biting and raping;

- Underreporting due to embarrassment, denial, or other factors;

Samples of battered women exist but:

Few researchers use control groups of non-battered women;

Most studies are conducted through shelters and therefore collect information only about women who seek this type of help and have chosen to leave, at least temporarily, the situation;

The size of the samples are usually small.

It has been difficult to study men who batter because:

- Many batterers deny they have a problem, refuse to recognize the seriousness of their acts, and rarely seek assistance.

- Those studies conducted generally utilize men at extreme ends of the continuum, in terms of seriousness or motivation. Men studied generally are mandated to treatment after arrest or conviction, generally for serious assaults or murder, or other men studied are those who voluntarily seek help;

- Few researchers use control groups;

- Many descriptive studies of men who batter use the reports of women who have been battered, which are subject to incomplete information and the perceptions of an affected party.

There are, however, some general observations about battering men and battered women that have emerged from the research that most authors and practitioners agree upon.

Battering occurs in all social groupings. It crosses all racial, ethnic, socioeconomic, religious, age and geographic boundaries. While Straus suggests that battering may be somewhat more frequent and severe in blue-collar homes than in upper income families, other studies do not replicate this and some repudiate it. In a later study Straus noted no class difference in a sample of college students who reported physical punishment or threat in their family of origin. Stark and McEvoy indicate that men with college educations are more likely to accept the use of violence in homes than those with fewer years of education. The educational achievement of battering men and battered women in Pagelow's study almost matches the national percentages of educational achievement.

Battered women are less likely than battering men to have witnessed their mothers being physically abused by their fathers and less likely to have been physically abused themselves as children than their partners. While battering men are more likely to have experienced violence in their families of origin than their women partners, only some studies suggest that this is to a greater extent than non-battering males. It is important to note that most battered women and battering men did not grow up in homes that they considered violent.

Battering appears to become more frequent, more serious, and more painful over time.[20] Although loss of control is often cited by perpetrators and therapists as a contributing factor in domestic violence, some studies point to the increasing control of, and perhaps greater learning of, violent techniques by men who batter. The type and location of injuries sustained suggest the use of violence to damage a woman's ego and control her interactions with others (facial injuries and disabling conditions) and to hide the use of force from public view (injuries to the trunk and internal injury).

No empirical evidence exists that either men who beat women, or women who are in relationship with men who batter, are mentally ill. Although men and women who could be labelled mentally ill may be perpetrators or victims, the percentage is likely to be that of the incidence in the general population.

The relationship of alcohol and other drugs to this type of family violence is unclear. While many battered women note that their assailants either were under the influence at the time of the incident, or that the man had an alcohol or drug problem, these factors have not been explored in relation to the reports that: 1) 5 to 10 percent of the general population has a serious alcohol problem, 2) alcohol or drug use has been utilized as a socially and legally acceptable mitigating factor in violent behavior, and 3) women victims may cite alcohol or drug abuse as causal in an attempt to understand or explain incomprehensible or unreasonable behavior.

Some general psychological attributes have been noted about the abuser and the abused. In this area particularly, the limitations of the research should be emphasized, as well as the tendency both to blame the victim and to seek simplistic answers. Most of the attributes can be accorded those persons on the end of a continuum of battering persons who have experienced battering that has been frequent and of relatively long duration. The psychological characteristics of the women who are battered may be developed or exacerbated by the dynamic of the battering relationship. They may also be the extreme expression of natural coping mechanisms. The psychological factors more typically associated with women who are battered are: fear, guilt, isolation, low self-esteem, a strong sense of responsibility and, occasionally, depressive characteristics. Men who batter are generally characterized as persons with low self-esteem, pathologically jealous, presenting a "dual personality," exhibiting limited coping ability, and severe stress reactions.

CAUSAL FACTORS: THEORIES

The theoretical perspective one chooses to explain the phenomenon of violence against women by their intimates determines the interventive strategies chosen to treat the woman and the male perpetrator; the social policies enacted to address the present problem; and the methods and goals established to prevent its future recurrence.

Most authors acknowledge that the problem of violence against women was subject to selective inattention by social scientists until the 1970s. As O'Brien notes in a 1971 article, " . . . in the Index for all editions of the *Journal of Marriage and the Family*, from its inception in 1939 through 1969, not a single article can be found which contains the word 'violence' in the title."[21] The lack of attention to the problem may indicate the general sexist nature of the society as well as values which excluded the exploration of violence between intimates. In fact, until the 1980s, the few articles that explored the nature of conflict between spouses generally "blamed the victim" for the battering. Authors tended to note the psychopathology of both individuals, in some situations blaming the males' aggressiveness on unduly controlling mothers. The women who were the victims of violence were variously characterized as masochistic, passive, aggressive, submissive, and controlling. All were seen as responsible for bringing the violence upon themselves.

Throughout the 1970s and 1980s a myriad of theories emerged to explain the phenomenon of violence in families. Straus attempted to categorize and integrate the major theories into a generalized systems theory and framework. His typology of the major theories explaining "spouse abuse" includes:[22]

> Intraindividual theories:
>   Psychopathology
>   Alcohol and drugs
> Sociopsychological theories:
>   Frustration-aggression
>   Social learning
>   Self-attitude
>   "Clockwork Orange"
>   Symbolic interaction
>   Exchange Theory
>   Attribution theory
> Sociocultural theories:
>   Functional
>   Culture of violence
>   Structural
>   General systems
>   Conflict
>   Resource

Another category that could be added might be titled *Feminist Theories*. The major proponents of such theories, such as Pagelow and the Dobashes, incorporate many aspects of other theories, especially the sociocultural theories. However, the primary critique offered of the general theories of family violence is their pretense of universal application to all humans and their failure to acknowledge the special conditions of women in this society. For instance, frustration-aggression theories hold that aggression is an innate response to blocked goals. These theories fail to account for the limited aggressive behaviors demonstrated by women within a cultural context that highly values economic achievement yet consistently denies women access to successful economic pathways. All of the general theories do not integrate the historical context of women in a patriarchal society; the economic oppression of women; their socialization to emotional attributes that are other than those of a mentally healthy adult, or their existence within institutions that systematically deny them equal power or protection. General system theories, for instance, recognize the role violence plays in maintaining homeostasis within the family system, but not recognize or acknowledge the oppression of women or children within that context.

The proponents of a feminist theory or feminist theories of violence against women generally utilize socio psychological or sociological approaches to explain the problem. Lenore Walker utilizes a social learning theory framework to explain the sense of helplessness and passivity which battered women experience following repeated battering. She asserts that the battered woman's inability to act on her own behalf is conditioned in the violent relationship but can be overcome when a woman successfully leaves the violent partner.

Mildred Pagelow studied 350 battered women who primarily were residents of shelters. Her study suggests that women who have few resources, receive negative institutional responses, and hold a traditional ideology concerning the role of women are more likely to remain in situations in which they have been battered. The Dobashes state that wives are deemed the "appropriate victims" of marital violence because of the historically and socially sanctioned primacy of the patriarchy in American and British cultures.

It is evident that no one factor can account for the complexities of a battering situation. A myriad of factors which operate in a dynamic environment both give rise to the violent episode and support the relationship of the individuals when violence is present. Additional research is needed from a feminist perspective, to assess the contributions of each theoretical area that will further our understanding of the phenomenon and prevent its continuation.

THE RESPONSE OF SYSTEMS TO BATTERED WOMEN

Now the first response which I myself think of is "Why didn't you seek help?"

I did. I went early in our marriage to a clergyman who after a few visits told me that my husband meant no real harm, he was just confused and felt insecure. I was to be more tolerant and understanding. Most important, I was to forgive him the beatings just as Christ had forgiven me from the Cross. I did.

Things continued. I turned this time to doctor. I was given little pills to relax me and told to take things a little easier. I was "just too nervous."

I turned to a friend and when her husband found out he accused me of either making things up or exaggerating the situation. She was told to stay away from me. (She didn't, but she could no longer help.)

I turned to a professional family guidance agency. I was told there that he needed help and I should find a way to control the incidents. I couldn't control the beating—that was his decision. I was asked to defend myself against suspicion that I wanted to be hit. I invited a beating. Good God! Did Jews invite themselves to be slaughtered in Germany?

I did go to doctors on two occasions. One asked me what I had done to provoke him and the other asked if we had "made up" yet.

I called the police one time. They not only didn't respond to the call, they called several hours later to ask if things had "settled down." I could have been dead by then!

I have nowhere to go if it happens again.[23]

The most commonly asked question about battered women is "Why does she stay?" Yet the reverse, "Why does *he* stay?" is rarely encountered. While most authors will agree that a combination of causal factors interact to keep women in relationships in spite of battering, such as the norms approving the use of violence and the submission of women based upon the historical and cultural antecedents, other practical and debilitating conditions also work to inhibit a woman from leaving her partner.

It should also be noted that severe battering and often murder occurs after a woman has separated from or divorced her partner. Therefore leaving may not unilaterally end battering. Fear for her own and her children's safety often works in conjunction with her belief that his behavior will change, and/or the reality that she has nowhere to go.

> 71 percent of the women in one study stated that their partner threatened to kill them if they left and 97 percent stated that at least on one occasion they feared that he would kill them.[24]

> Most studies report that the majority of women had sought help from at least one source prior to leaving an abusive situation.

> Pagelow reports that 42 percent of the women she studied had attempted to leave the abuse four or more times prior to the present attempt.[25]

While some women have limited access to "legitimate" resources, such as cash, a supportive network of family or friends, or strong assertive and communication skills, to assist them in leaving an abusive partner, almost all battered women seek help from traditional institutions or systems. The medical, mental health, and criminal justice/legal systems are the traditional formal sources of assistance sought by battered women. Yet each of these systems has reflected the pervasive cultural myths and stereotypes about battering and have generally been unresponsive to the needs of battered women.

The Medical System

Most authors and practitioners note that the majority of battered women have sought medical attention at least once for injuries suffered from their husbands or partners. In Pagelow's study, almost one-third of the women interviewed said they needed medical attention but didn't get it, and most (44 percent) gave the reason that their abuser refused to let them go.

For those women who do seek medical attention, especially on repeated occasions, this help-giving avenue may do nothing to address the source of the injury and may in fact compound the violence she experiences in her relationship. Statistics from Boston City Hospital record that approximately 70 percent of the assault victims received in its emergency room are known to be women who have been attacked in their homes, usually by a lover or husband.[26] Eva Stark and Anne Flitcrat in ongoing research at Yale-New Haven Hospital note the following:

> Battering accounts for almost one in every five visits by women to the emergency trauma service.
>
> Almost one-half of all injuries reported to this service occur within the context of ongoing abuse.
>
> Battering accounted for nearly one in every four suicide attempts by all women.
>
> Battered women were significantly more likely to be receiving prescriptions for analgesics and minor tranquilizers.[27]

Stark's critique of the medical system states that its clinical response to battered women has become integrated into the "battering syndrome." Specifically, he asserts that because medical personnel ignore battering as a woman's primary problem and treat a woman's injuries or complaints symptomatically, they unwittingly foster a cycle in which the woman is encouraged to accept responsibility for the battering and perpetuate her continuing abuse.

Mental Health

> There are two definitions of woman. There is the good woman. She is a victim. There is the bad woman. She must be destroyed.
>
> . . . There is the good woman. She is the victim. The posture of victimization, the passivity of the victim demands abuse.
>
> Women strive for passivity, because women want to be good. The abuse provoked by that passivity convinces women that they are bad. . . .[28]

A psychiatrist, marriage counselor, therapist, or counselor is chosen by some battered women as a source of support, reality testing, or advice. Although some women have indicated that they sought such help, they also noted that their attempts were often frustrated by husbands/partners who refuse to accompany them (to marriage counseling, for instance) or refuse to allow them to go. Many women seek such help without acknowledging to the care giver the physical abuse present in their relationship.

Generally, mental health workers do not seek out such information. The phenomenon of sex-role stereotyping within the mental health professions so well documented by Broverman et al. often reinforces a woman's role as victim. This classic study showed that clinicians accepted a notion of mental health which demanded a person's adjustment to norms of behavior appropriate for one's sex, regardless of how this behavior matches a standard for normal, healthy adult functioning. While the expectations for male behavior closely matched that of a healthy adult, the concept of behavior ascribed to women was considerably less healthy. Those characteristics valued as healthy for an adult female included: very dependent, very passive, very home-oriented, and not at all self-confident.[29] While these characteristics are the extreme of a bipolar system, and while later studies suggest a movement in the mental health professions to a more androgynous standard of mental health, sex-role stereotyping remains a major cause of concern for all women, but especially for battered women.

For battered women seeking help, the double standard of mental health and the common emphasis on maintaining a family system "in spite of conflict" encourages them to remain in a battering situation. In addition, the perception that battering is an intrapsychic or family dynamics problem continues to encourage women to nurture a battering man and to believe that he will "change." Many therapists and counselors ascribing to such beliefs and with limited training about and fear of violence, exacerbate the problem. For those men who do seek help, and estimates are that this is an extremely small percentage, the clinical emphasis upon ego strength, frustration tolerance, or self-esteem, diverts attention from the most serious problem: the violent behavior.

While the mental health professions have the skills and stated values that could reduce the incidence of violence against women by intimates, only a few of its practitioners have been willing to resolutely label it a problem and develop workable strategies for both women and men.

The Legal and Criminal Justice Systems

> In 1874 the Supreme Court of North Carolina nullified a husband's right to chastise his wife "under any circumstances." But the court's ruling became ambiguous when it added, "if no permanent injury has been inflicted, nor malice, cruelty, nor dangerous violence shown by the husband, it is better to draw the curtain, shut out the public gaze, and leave the parties to forgive and forget.[30]

This ruling became the basis for the American legal system in the nineteenth and twentieth centuries. Civil and criminal law and related procedures and rulings have systematically denied battered women equal protection and due process.[31] Vestiges of the treatment of women as property of their husbands remain even into the present, with most states denying women the ability to charge their husbands with rape or to collect damages from him for injuries sustained. Battered women have been viewed as persons who have brought their victimization upon themselves and persons who are "appropriately" disciplined by the males in relation to them.

Usually, from the first encounter with the system, in calling the police, battered women have faced a dual standard of justice. The procedural emphasis upon "cooling off" the situation rather than arrest of the perpetrator heightens the danger to the woman and increases the likelihood of further violence. A study conducted in Kansas City demonstrated that in 85 percent of the female homicides, the police had been called to that address at least once in the previous year, and in 50 percent of these homicides, they had been summoned five or more times.[32] In spite of the seriousness of such "domestic" calls to the police (more police are killed in the line of duty responding to such calls than to any other type of call) and the frequency, (they are the largest single category of call) the response of the police has generally been inadequate. The lack of availability of protection to victims and consequences to perpetrators allows violence to escalate and reinforces a woman's belief that help is not available. In a landmark ruling in Connecticut it has been determined that a battered woman's civil rights have been violated in the lack of equal protection afforded her by police.

From the earliest point of entry into the system, police intervention, through prosecution, conviction, and sentencing, the criminal justice system has reflected wider cultural norms approving "wife-battering" to some tolerable limit, usually something short of murder. Yet even murder may not be dealt with severely in that sentences are based upon not only the convicted charge (usually lessened in the case of husbands/partners murdering their wives because of the emotionally mitigating circumstances) but also an assessment of dangerousness, which includes an assessment of prior convictions of assaults to other than family members, employment history, and the like.

In a study conducted by Faulk of 23 men charged with seriously assaulting or murdering their wives or "cohabitees," it was found that none of eight charged were found guilty of murder; only one received a sentence of over 5 years; and almost 30 percent of those convicted received noncustodial sentences.[33] Although the criminal justice system has been justifiably criticized for its repressive use of social control functions against the poor and minorities, an equitable application of control mechanisms exerted against battering males could reduce the incidence.

Social Work

Because social workers practice in a broad spectrum of the public and private sectors, they as a group have enormous potential for impact on the problem of violence against women. Working in criminal justice, education, mental health, health, public policy, legislative, or other roles, social workers can identify women who have been abused; assist them and their children; exert control over the behaviors of battering men; and establish policy to prevent woman abuse. Social work as a profession, however, has had a somewhat blemished history in respect to the problem.

Certainly the profound influence of Freud and the psychotherapeutic bias of the profession has negatively affected battered women as individuals and as a group. The criticism offered by Susan

Schechter of the former president of the National Association of Social Workers echoes a continual threat sensed by many workers in the shelter movement that the "professionalization" of services to battered women and their children may remove the focus of empowerment and feminist social change which characterize the grass root approach to service. It is specifically the failure to mention the grass roots and feminist efforts which brought about services to battered women that impelled Schechter to comment that the president's "statement rewrites the history of the battered women's movement."[34]

A number of the elements of social work that are said to enhance or "professionalize" the work, in fact detract from its ability adequately to assist battered women. Because the interventions chosen to address any social problem must, to be effective, reflect the etiology of the problem, social work must address not just the individual woman or man, or their family unit, but must address them within a societal and cultural context.

1.   The emphasis upon the development of a common language fosters the use of the term *victim* for battered women, which limits our understanding of the dynamics of repeated victimization and denies their courage.

2.   The emphasis upon scientific research ignores the context in which battering takes place and minimizes the importance of research, such as qualitative research, which may be better able to assist in our understanding of the phenomenon.

3.   The importance of personal and professional credibility reduces the level of systems pressure which can be exerted to create change and limits community organizing tactics.

4.   The pressure for accountability moves organizations to impose hierarchical, nonparticipatory, and oppressive conditions for workers which mirror the abusive relationship.

Social workers also exist within their cultural context, a society which legitimizes battering. In an unpublished study conducted in a graduate school of social work, it was found that one-third of the students approved of slapping a spouse under certain circumstances. As members of any occupation, social workers also batter women.

Social workers have, however, made significant contributions to the battered women's movement. The social-work value base, helping and community organizing skills, understanding of the individual within an environmental context, and ethical standards have supported and enhanced the work of shelter providers and activists. Ginny NiCarthy's self-help guide for women in abusive situations, and Susan Schechter's history of the battered women's movement in the United States, which illuminates its political and ideological foundations and challenges, are two examples of the major positive contributions that social workers have made to the battered women's movement. Social workers have also worked throughout the movement providing direct service, consultation, administration, legislative advocacy, training, and community organizing.

But there is more to be done. As a helping profession, it is social work's responsibility to understand the social problem and the needs of the affected individuals from the group's perspective. It has an obligation to assure that social benefits and controls are distributed equitably. As a profession which is entrusted to review the conduct of its members, it must assure that violence against women in any fashion is neither promoted nor ignored in its activities.

As an individual social worker, one must understand the ethical obligations in practice. Specifically, if as a social worker one cannot *unequivocally* reject the use of force and violence in interpersonal relationships, then one has an obligation to remove oneself from practice situations in which this value must be exercised. In choosing to work in the field of "family violence," which includes child abuse, many particular skills must be learned. All social workers, however, who wish to make a contribution to the battered women's movement may do so in the personal, political, or professional arena. Some examples of help and prevention efforts are to:

- Be able to identify possible battered women and battering men in your practice.
- Provide safe, positive, and crisis help for women who are battered.
- Know the most effective and available local resources: shelters, support groups, hot lines, advocates, etc.
- Explore and understand the actual danger that a woman is in; empathize with the emotional turmoil and constraints promoted by battering; recognize and reinforce the battered women's courage and strength.

- Acknowledge your rejection of the use of violence under any circumstances.
- Set clear and realistic limits with men who batter or may be suspected of battering. Acknowledge the limits of confidentiality if a threat is stated.
- Advocate for changes in the criminal justice system that recognize the seriousness of personal, rather than property crime, and acknowledge the importance of crime against women regardless of the relationship with the perpetrator.
- Promote the rights of all victims (sic) within the criminal justice system that work in concert with the civil liberties of all.
- Lobby for legislative protection for battered women including enforceable protective orders, the recognition of marital rape, and mandatory police training.
- Demand adequate funding for services for battered women and their children, including shelters and legal protection.
- Promote sex-role equality and economic equality for women. Assure adequate child support.
- Work to eliminate the use of violence in child rearing.
- Work to eliminate violence on a national level.

NOTES

1. Straus, M., Wife beating: How common and why? *Victimology*, 2(3–4), 445.
2. Idem., 447.
3. *Crimes of violence*, A Staff Report to the National Commission on the Causes and Prevention of Violence, Washington, D.C., U.S. Government Printing Office, 1969, 360.
4. Leghorn, L. *Social responses to battered women*, A report presented to the Wisconsin Conference on Battered Women, 1976.
5. Dobash, R. E. & Dobash, R. *Violence against wives*, New York: Free Press, 1979; 40.
6. Brownmiller, S. *Against our will*, New York: Pathfinder Press, 1970, 16.
7. Eisenberg, S., & Micklow, P., The assaulted wife: Catch 22 revisited, Rutgers University School of Law, 1974, 11.

8. Dobash, ibid., 98.

9. Straus, ibid., 447.

10. Gauquin, D. A., Spouse abuse: Data from the National Crime Survey, *Victimology* 2(3-4), 640.

11. *California homicides*, 1971.

12. Dobash, ibid., 246.

13. Fields, M. Wife beating: Government intervention policies and practices, *Battered Women: Issues of Public Policy*, A Consultation sponsored by the United States Civil Rights Commission, 1978, 20.

14. Straus, ibid., 449.

15. Pagelow, M. *Woman-battering*, Beverly Hills: Sage Publications, 1981, 24.

16. Dobash, ibid., 17.

17. *11 Crimes of Violence*, Staff Report to the National Commission on the Causes and Prevention of Violence, 1969, 360.

18. Wolfgang, M. E. *Patterns in criminal homicide*, New York: Wiley, 1958, 217.

19. Fields, ibid., 26.

20. Pagelow, ibid., 163.

21. O'Brien, J. E. Violence in divorce prone families, *Journal of Marriage and the Family*, November 1971, *33* 692.

22. Gelles, R. J. & Straus, M. A. Determinants of violence in the family: Toward a theoretical integration. In W. R. Burr, et al. (Eds.), *Contemporary theories about the family*, New York: Free Press, 1977, 560-561.

23. Anonymous, Letter received by Marta Segovia Ashley and submitted as testimony to the United States Commission on Human Rights. *Battered women: Issues of public policy, 1978, 373.*

24. *Rounsaville, B. J. Theories in marital violence from a study of battered women, Victimology, 3(1-2), 16.*

25. Pagelow, ibid., 72.

26. Warrior, B., Battered lives, In Leghorn, L. & Warrior, B. *Houseworker's Handbook*, Cambridge, MA, 1975, 25.

27. Stark, E. & Flitcraft, A. Medical therapy as repression: The case of the battered woman, *Health and Medicine*, Summer/Fall, 1982, *31*.

28. Dworkin, A. *Woman hating*, New York: E. P. Dutton, 1976, 55.

29. Broverman, I. et al., Sex-role stereotypes and clinical judgments of mental health. *Journal of Consulting and Clinical Psychology, 34*(1), 3.

30. Del Martin, *Battered wives*, San Francisco, CA: Glide Publications, 1976, 32.
31. Fields, ibid., 21.
32. Kansas City, Missouri Police Department, *Domestic Violence and the Police*, Unpublished report, 1973.
33. Faulk, M. Men who assault their wives, *Medicine, Science, and the Law*, 1974, *14*, 181.
34. Schechter, S. *Women and male violence*, Boston: South End Press, 1982, 3.

Chapter 6

CHILD ABUSE AND FAMILY VIOLENCE
Julia Hamilton

"He walked into a cigarette." This unlikely history of an infant with burns of the upper eyelid and cornea brings glances of evident frustrations around the conference table, where social workers, doctors, and nurses are gathered. The report continues, "he has two siblings, both with histories of abuse. Mother addicted to cocaine. All live intermittently with the maternal grandmother."

This report is one of 10 given in a weekly conference at a major teaching hospital. Other reports deal with a newborn baby who can't go home, such incidents as a serious fracture, possible neglect, and emotional abuse. Each story is a sad and unique tangle of the elements of family life. But the burned infant represents a particularly frustrating failure to protect a child born into a family with other children known to be "at risk."

"It shouldn't hurt to be a child." Nevertheless, a million children, maybe more, are victims of abuse every year. Countless adults are trapped by their history into acts of social violence. That's one way to look at the problem of child abuse. But there's another. Child abuse comes down to one child who is physically injured; one child who is deprived of what he or she needs to thrive; one child who is exploited for the sexual gratification of an adult; one child who is made to feel unloved—small, worthless, and no good.

Historically, society has been troubled by the maltreatment of children. When children were not wanted, infant mortality rates were high. In nineteenth century London, 80 percent of the illegitimate children were given to nurses to raise; often these women collected their fees and then promptly killed the babies.[1] When a profit could be made, adults sometimes sold children into slavery; or often used them as a source of cheap labor. Certainly most parents had concern for their own children; but pervasive values sanctioned many practices that we now call abusive and even caring parents followed profit-making practices.

Mutilation of children is usually presumed to be a very remote custom of olden times. Examples such as the foot-binding of Chinese daughters and the cranial deformations of certain Indian groups are well known. Mutilation of sexual organs is still seen as a religious rite in some African tribes, and though the value of circumcision is questioned, it is certainly common in western medicine today.[2]

In order to understand the emerging awareness of child abuse, as any other social issue, such as women's suffrage or the civil rights of minorities, it is necessary to understand the history of child welfare. "Spare the rod and spoil the child" was a theme supported by the Bible and expressed in 1633 in *Bibliotheca Scholastica*. Beatings to drive out the devil were a form of therapeutic treatment especially applicable to children. Epileptic attacks were attributed to possession by the devil.

Children were seen as property of their parents and could be treated accordingly. Harsh treatment by parents was justified by the belief that severe physical punishment was necessary to maintain discipline, transmit educational decisions, and expel evil spirits.

The change in cultural values can be traced to the early days of the child welfare movement in the United States. The Children's Aid Society removed children from New York City's crowded slums and sent them west with families going to California in the 1840s and 1850s. In New York in 1925, the New York Society for the Reformation of Juvenile Delinquents established a house of refuge, primarily for "wayward" children and secondarily for neglected and abused children. By 1961, knowledge had progressed to the degree that C. Henry Kempe arranged for an interdisciplinary presentation at the Annual Meeting of the American Academy of

Pediatrics on the subject of the battered child syndrome. Since 1962 literally thousands of articles and dozens of books have added to the understanding of child abuse and neglect. Sexual abuse of children became the hot topic in the late 1970s. The history of the emergence of child abuse as a social issue involves a growing recognition of this maltreatment plus the technical capability of professionals to trace clues that tell the history of inflicted injuries (use of X rays, etc.). There is also the readiness of society finally to address this problem in a constructive manner.

The National Committee for Prevention of Child Abuse defines child abuse as an injury or a pattern of injuries to a child that is nonaccidental. Child abuse includes nonaccidental physical injury, physical neglect, sexual abuse, and emotional abuse. "Child" means a person under the age of eighteen. An "abused or neglected child" means a child whose physical or mental health or welfare is harmed or threatened with harm by the acts or omissions of his parents or other persons responsible for his welfare.

Nonaccidental physical injury may include severe beatings, burns, immersion in scalding water, or human bites, with resultant bruises and welts, broken bones, scars, or serious internal injuries.

Physical neglect is the withholding of or failure to provide a child with the basic necessities of life: food, clothing, shelter, medical care, attention to hygiene, or supervision needed for optimal physical growth and development.

Sexual abuse is the exploitation of a child for the sexual gratification of an adult. It may range from exhibitionism and fondling to intercourse or use of a child in the production of pornographic materials. This form of abuse has escalated over the last 2 years.

Emotional abuse includes excessive, aggressive, or unreason able parental demands that place expectation on a child beyond their capabilities. Emotional abuse can show itself in constant and persistent teasing, belittling, or verbal attacks. Emotional abuse also includes failure to provide the psychological nurturance necessary for the child's psychological growth and development. Absence of love, care, support, and guidance presents emotional abuse.

Child abuse is not usually just one physical attack or just one instance of failure to meet a child's most basic needs. Usually child abuse is a pattern of behavior. It takes place over a period of time, and its effects add up. The longer child abuse continues, the more serious is the injury to the child, and the more difficult it is to stop.

This chapter examines child abuse in the context of violence in the family. Its main purpose is to offer social workers a framework for providing intervention and treatment for children and families who are experiencing abuse. By seeing the abuse of children as but one aspect of the more general dynamic of family violence, social workers may be better able to diagnose and treat carefully and completely children at risk. Further, the etiology of child abuse is more easily understood by placing abuse within the context of family violence.

VIOLENCE TOWARD CHILDREN AND VIOLENCE IN THE HOME

Estimates of the extent of child abuse have ranged from thousands of cases to tens of thousands, to hundreds of thousands, to millions. These estimates are based on officially reported cases of child abuse, which is the cause of their variability. Variation is the result of these facts:

1. The laws mandating reporting of child abuse have changed over the years. For example, Gil's research, which revealed some 6,000 officially reported and valid cases of child abuse in 1967 has to be understood in light of the fact that laws mandating the reporting of child abuse had not been passed in all 50 states at that time.
2. The definition of abuse may vary from one professional group to another.
3. Not all instances of child abuse come to public or official attention.[3]

Official statistics on child abuse and other forms of family violence reflect the workings of the official system as it attempts to measure the extent of abuse.

While perhaps underestimating the true level of violence in the American family, the available official statistics do indicate that the family is perhaps society's most violent institution. Americans are more likely to be murdered in their homes by members of their families than anywhere else. It is also estimated that 2,000 to 5,000 children are killed each year by their parents, although these figures probably underestimate the true incidence of child mortality rate, as many cases are labeled "accidents" rather than homicides.[4]

FORMS OF VIOLENCE TOWARD CHILDREN

The milder forms of violence toward children are, of course, the most common. Of the 1,146 individuals who had at least one child between the ages of three and seventeen living at home (children under three years of age were excluded because the survey by Gil also investigated violence among siblings) 58 percent had performed some act of violence toward their child during the survey year; 71 percent had done so at some time in the course of raising the child.

Of greater interest are the age differences. Among the three and four-year-olds, and also among the five to nine-year-olds, 82 percent had been hit during the year of the survey. Two-thirds (66 percent) of the preteens and early teenage children (ten to fourteen-year-olds) had been hit that year. Of the fifteen to seventeen-year-olds, one-third, 34 percent, had been hit by their parents. The striking of children thus is certainly not confined only to young children.[5]

The most dangerous types of violence occurred less often. Even for these extreme types of violence, however, there proved an astonishingly high number of American children who were kicked, punched, bitten, threatened with a gun or knife, or had guns or knives used against them.

Such acts of violence not only affect a large number of children but, on the average, happen more than once a year. These extreme forms of parental violence occur periodically and even regularly in the families where they occur at all.

FACTORS ASSOCIATED WITH FAMILY VIOLENCE

Early research and writing on child abuse and family violence was dominated by the *psychopathological model*. Child abuse researchers discounted social factors as playing any causal role in violence toward children. Rather, the explanation was thought to lie in personality or character disorders of individual battering parents. The exception to this point of view was Gil's multi-dimensional model of child abuse, which placed heavy emphasis on factors such as inequality and poverty.

Both medically and socioscientifically oriented researchers appear at present to agree that fewer than 10 percent of the incidents of child abuse and domestic violence can be attributed solely to personality factors of the batterers.

The current conceptual model used to examine and explain family violence considers the interplay of both psychological and social factors. Current research indicates that a number of factors are associated with child abuse, and family violence:

1.   The cycle of violence: Violence begets violence has been the hypothesis for many years. One of the consistent conclusions of research on child abuse and domestic violence is that individuals who have experienced violent and abusive childhoods are more likely to grow up to become child and spouse abusers than individuals who experienced little or no violence in their childhood years. Steinmetz reports that even less severe forms of violence are passed on from generation to generation.

2.   Socioeconomic status: Some research on family violence supports the hypothesis that domestic violence is more prevalent in families of low socioeconomic status. This conclusion, however, does not mean that domestic violence is *confined* to lower-class households. Investigators reporting the differentials distribution of violence are frequently careful to point out that child and spouse abuse can be found in families across the spectrum of socioeconomic status. Nevertheless, many of the reports only reflect the low socioeconomic class. This is possible because police and hospital emergency room statistics are from this class primarily.

3.   Stress: A third consistent finding of most domestic violence research is that rates of family violence are directly related to social stress in families. Investigators report associations between various forms of family violence and specific stressful situations and conditions, such as 1) unemployment or part-time employment of males, 2) financial problems, 3) pregnancy, and 4) single-parent families.

4. Social Isolation: A fourth major finding in the study of both child and spouse abuse is that social isolation raised the risk of severe violence directed at children or between spouses.

In the case of violence toward children, some of the factors are:

1. Larger than average size family.
2. Low birth weight of child.
3. Prematurity of child.
4. Lack of attachment between mother and child, sometimes correlated with low birth weight or prematurity.

In addition, females are found to be slightly more likely to abuse their children, and males are slightly more likely to be victims of child abuse. Lastly, researchers have proposed that handicapped, retarded, or developmentally delayed children, or children perceived by their parents as "different," are at risk of being abused.

CAUTIONS IN ASSESSING FACTORS RELATED TO CHILD ABUSE AND FAMILY VIOLENCE

1. Even though cross-generalization patterns of violence do exist, many researchers believe this theory is overstated.[6] There are other factors such as the environment and the individual's ability to adjust to his environment that must be considered.

2. For instance, while most investigators find stress, isolation, and history of violence statistically related to family violence, the associations have not been sufficient to allow a researcher or practitioner to use any one of these factors to predict or explain child abuse and family violence. While many clinicians and researchers search for simple answers to the complex problems of family violence, the research to date all to clearly points out that single-factor explanations of child abuse and family violence are inadequate, inaccurate, and misleading.

3. Most research on child abuse and family violence draws cases for study from official records, social agencies, police files, or hospitals. By examining only those cases of violence and abuse that come to public attention, researchers are unable to determine if the factors they find associated with violence and abuse are causal factors or factors that lead a family to be identified as abusive.

For example, are single-parent, low-income families more likely to abuse their children, or are they, because of their vulnerable status, more likely to have the injuries of their children correctly or incorrectly diagnosed as abuse? This is an important question for both clinician and researchers. It becomes more crucial in the diagnosis and treatment of suspected abuse and violence victims and it forces social workers and others to think about the kind of treatment they are providing to parents who are abusive.

CASE ILLUSTRATIONS

Mike and Janet had their first baby, a boy, as the result of a pregnancy which was instrumental in leading them to get married. Unfortunately, this otherwise quite healthy little boy was born with a congenital stricture of the bladder neck which required two long hospitalizations with surgery during the first 6 months of his life. Not surprisingly, he was a fussy, whiny, difficult-to-care-for baby, requiring much more than average care and offering less happy, rewarding behavioral response to his parents.

When he was 8 months old, his father returned home late from an unusually hard day at work and found his wife terribly upset and irritable because of conflicts between her and his mother. His wife, in an effort to assuage her own turmoil, left the baby with her husband and went to visit her own mother. Mike, tired, feeling quite needy, deserted by Janet, was faced with caring for a crying baby. After several attempts to comfort and feed the baby, he lost all patience and struck the infant, fracturing its skull. Fortunately, there were no serious consequences from this major injury.

Mike came under our care some 5 years later because of his worry over the fact that he was still very punitive toward John, and often spanked and slapped him. By this time, a second boy, Jason, had been born and was now ten months old. Mike spoke of his attitude toward Jason being entirely different, and when asked why, responded, "Well, Jason's just the kind of a kid I like. Whenever I want to play with him, he plays. He does everything that I want him to do."

This case clearly describes an infant born as the result of a premaritally conceived pregnancy, or who comes as an accident too soon after the birth of a previous child, perhaps unwelcome to the parents and who starts life under the cloud of being unrewarding and unsatisfying to the parents.

Babies are born with quite different behavior patterns: Many parents are hurt and disappointed when they have a very placid child instead of a hoped-for more reactive, responsive baby. Other parents are equally distressed by having an active, aggressive baby who makes up his own mind, when they had hoped for a very clinging, compliant infant. A potent source of difficulty is the situation in which babies are born with some degree of congenital defect, therefore requiring much more medical as well as general care. Thus, it is obvious that characteristics presented by the infant such as sex, time of birth, health status, and behavior are factors in instigating child abuse. Obviously, the unwitting contributions that infants make toward the disappointments and burdens of their parents can hardly be used as an excuse for child abuse. The essence of the problem is the excessive demands that parents impose upon infants, disregarding the ability of the infants to meet them.

The following case history illustrates the occurrence of sexual abuse of a child in the home environment:

Bob K. is a white male, two years and two months old. He is the son of Betty and Robert K., both 22 years old. The couple have been married 4 years; Bob is their only child. Both parents reside in the home, and have extended family on both sides who reside in the area.

Bob was referred to the clinic for a sexual abuse evaluation. The referral was precipitated by a referral made to DCYS by the parents' neighbors. The referral to DCYS stated that the child had been heard to complain that his "hinie" hurt and that his daddy had done it. Neighbors also complained that the father exhibited other sexual problems; e.g., he had drilled holes in walls to peep into their apartments, he distributed pornography, and had exposed himself. DCYS made a home visit to the family and spoke with the mother. Ms. K was aware of her husband's other sexual activities, but was not aware of any sexual misuse of their son. However, she had been concerned for her son's welfare for the past year because of his father's other activities. She does not permit the boy to spend time alone with his father, and has not permitted them to be alone for at least the last 9 months. She has confronted her husband about his sexual activities, but not about any possible misuse of the boy.

The child's grandfather told Ms. K that her husband had been accused of child molestation as a teenager, but that the charges were apparently dropped. This information caused Ms. K even more concern for her son's welfare. Ms. K stated that she had not noticed any tension between her son and his father. She does have some concerns about her son's sexual development, however. She noted that he seems to rub his penis a lot, and will often stick his finger in his rectum or stick other objects in it; on one occasion he stuck a stereo clip in his rectum.

Ms. K is very concerned about her husband and her son. She is very anxious to get help for her husband, but is afraid to approach him. She says he had a bad temper and has hit her occasionally. She is afraid he will respond with anger and possibly violence if he finds out.

Children are easily seduced by someone whom they have learned to trust and to look to for guidance. Oral copulation, masturbation, and genital manipulation are presented as love, fun, or "their secret." The child often experiences bodily pleasure as well as feelings of power—the child and one parent sharing a secret and a special relationship that they hide from the other parent. The child becomes "special" and is treated differently by the father. The roles and alliances within the family become more confused. The father is the authority with power, and he is also the child's lover. The mother is feeling confused and afraid about how to handle her feelings toward the father. She is angry and hurt about her husband's behavior and she is afraid for her child.

The social worker needs to explore with the mother all her confused and angry feelings toward the father, and help the mother confront the father about what has happened to the child. The social worker should also engage the child in a doll-play session in order to allow the child a chance to express through play what has happened to him or her. Often parents meet in groups to get support for breaking up their families or having their mates arrested.

Such a case will engage the social worker in extending treatment to the entire family system in order to involve the father. The primary focus in these sessions would be the couple's relationship: how they were coping with living together since the disclosure, how they dealt with the loneliness in their relationship, and how they react to those in their respective families who are now aware of the incestuous behavior. The purpose of the session would be to break through the denial process.

Suzanne Sgroi, a specialist in child sexual abuse, does not believe that the pattern of sexually abusing children can be changed voluntarily. The social worker or therapist needs to use the criminal justice system and child protective agencies to investigate and validate the complaint. With their authority, the clinician then has power to deal with the abuser. There is also protection for the child. It is essential to the clinician that the clients know that she or he has been given this power by legal agencies.

From the victim's viewpoint, the child or grown-up victim needs to be helped to know that they were powerless. They need to be relieved of guilt, to know they were not responsible for the abuse, and could not have prevented it. They need to admit exactly what happened and to be relieved of any self-blame. It is important to restore their self-esteem. Group therapy is a method that is successful for both the victims and the child abusers. Individual treatment is also necessary.[7]

THE ROLE OF THE SOCIAL WORKER IN CHILD ABUSE CASES

Social workers first need to ask themselves the following questions: What are people like who severely beat or sexually abuse children? How do they appear to others, and how do they appear to themselves? What, if anything, makes them different from other human beings? How can we go about improving the lives of the adults and children who lived in the remarkably volatile and dangerous situation that led to child abuse?

Abusing parents usually want the child to be sensitive to *their* needs. One mother had a full day of hysterics because her daughter did not keep her coat on while she was outdoors. Above all things, the parents must feel in control of the child. Children are considered to exist as sources of gratification by their battering parents.

The significance of what has been said about parental attitudes toward abused children and its relationship to treatment becomes evident when one realizes that these parents treat their children as they were treated as children. Many parents have had the impossible expected of them, with their needs always secondary to their own parents' needs. They were not recognized as distinct human beings with needs, wishes, and desires of their own. And because no child can accede to this, these parents grow up feeling that they have lived lives of failure and that they are now completely incompetent. They usually expect others to criticize them, to outrank them, to show their superiority over them and to leave them feeling more helpless than ever. Whatever they do, they will never make the mark and attain parental approval.

When a child beater is discovered by social workers, doctors, or others, it becomes apparent that these parents are extremely difficult people to reach. The person discovered harming his child fears punishment. He or she fears punishment because he views his environment as hostile and punitive. Parents feel uncomfortable about hurting their child because they sense environmental disapproval, and also, part of their own being disapproves of what they have done.

One mother who feared she would beat her child to death expressed her own feelings about her behavior this way; "Although I love her very much, my nervousness leads me to do things which I often disapprove of at the time, and if I don't disapprove of my actions at the time, I frequently disapprove of them later." She went on to say; "Many times after I beat her, she would lie in her crib and cry herself to sleep. I would sit next to the crib and cry and wish I could beat myself."

Most of the mothers that social workers deal with talk openly about needing the mothering they had never had before. They would use the social worker as the mother they always wanted. It is essential that the social worker give total interest to the patient. This is not easy, particularly when the patient is giving back a great deal of confused information. *Attention* is one gift that abusers appreciate receiving and it can be an ongoing gift because it eventually can be used by the patients themselves by turning it to their own advantage as they learn to pay attention to others, particularly their own children.

Some basic characteristics necessary for social workers who work with abusive parents are:

1. A strong working knowledge of child behavior/child development that can be shared with abusive parents at appropriate times;

2. Few, if any, managerial tendencies;

3. Willingness to put oneself out for patients, but without sacrificing oneself to everyone's discomfort;

4. The presence of satisfactions in life besides the job so that one won't be looking to the patient to provide these satisfactions;

5. Belief that parents can change and that with treatment, support, and encouragement they can become better parents;

6. Having experienced good mothering from their parent; and willingness to share those good feelings with the patient.

7. Willingness to look openly at one's own feelings toward abuse, and examine them with others in order to provide appropriate treatment to the patient.

Working with abusive parents can be very painful, and you will make some mistakes. Nevertheless, working with abusive parents can be a challenge, and not only will you help the parents, but you will provide a service that will have a lasting effect on families and children.

RECOMMENDATIONS FOR TRAINING OF SOCIAL WORKERS

Social workers should provide the treatment for the parents who are child abusers and for the children who are the victims. In order to provide services to this population, social workers need to understand the needs of their clients. They need to have the perspective that abusers can be of many types—rich, poor, highly intelligent, or of low intelligence and little education. They may be highly religious or have no religion. Their occupations cover a wide range from prestigious, high-paying jobs to unemployed. There can be many children in a family or only one. Their relationship to the abused child is one in which they are responsible for the child care and, as such, they may be parents, relatives, foster parents, or even babysitters.

The social worker needs to view the child abuser using intuition since there is no typical case or scientific certainty about the cause. If they understand that, they will individualize each client and realize that the abusing parent has human needs and must be approached with warmth and understanding. This can be very difficult for many social workers and they need to cultivate self-awareness regarding their own values and attitudes about child abuse. They must come to understand that the abusing parent often does not see the child as an immature human being without the ability to respond to the adult's expectations. Attitudinal training of social workers is important in that it should allow the workers to express their own feelings towards the abusing adult and reveal when these attitudes hinder the worker's ability to provide treatment to the abusers. The ability of social workers to reach out with empathy, to capitalize on whatever they have in common with their client, is very important. Any hint of rejection will damage the client relationship and child abusers are often very fragile human beings.

It is important that social workers know the laws about child abuse and have an understanding of the court system and how it can be helpful to social workers both on behalf of the child and the offender. It is also important that social workers participate on a national level in policy-making and in implementing laws that will provide help for both the victim and the offender who are trapped in the web of child abuse.

NOTES

1. Helfer, & Kemple, *The battered child*, (2nd ed.). Chicago, IL: University of Chicago Press, 1968.
2. Gil, D. G. *Violence against children*, Cambridge, MA: Harvard University Press, 1973. pp. 1–30.
3. Kempe, C. E., & Helfer, R. *Helping the battered child and his family*, Philadelphia, PA: Lippincott, 1972.
4. Fontana, U. J., *Somewhere a child is crying*, New York: Macmillan, 1973.

5. Young, L. *Wednesday's children: A study of child neglect and abuse.* New York: McGraw-Hill, 1964.
6. *National Child Protection Newsletter,* National Center for the Prevention and Treatment of Child Abuse and Neglect, 1001 Jasmine Street, Denver, Colorado.
7. Sgroi, S., Paper presented at Connecticut Human Services Conference, Meriden, November 20, 1986.

Chapter 7

"GRANNY-BASHING:"
Abuse of the Elderly

Frank O'Connor

HISTORICAL AND SOCIAL BACKGROUND

During the past 2 decades, violence within the family has become recognized as a major social problem. This fact seems related more to cultural value shifts involving both the role of the family in society as well as attitudes about aggressive behavior than to any increase in the incidence of violent acts between family members. Of interest is the evolution of societal awareness of the various classifications of family violence: a typology based upon identification of victims versus perpetrators. The most vulnerable victims—children of parental perpetrators of violence—were first to be identified and aided by social agencies and by the medical and legal professions. Later, mainly in the past decade, wives battered by husbands were labeled as a legitimate problem, in stark contrast to this phenomenon previously being seen as culturally normal.

Yet it has only been in the mid-1980s that two other types of family violence have been brought to the forefront: parent and grandparent abuse. "Granny-bashing" and "Gram-slamming," as some have labeled abuse of elderly parents, appears to be related to the other types of family violence in that the victim is usually psychologically, physically, and economically dependent on the aggressive offender, usually the adult offspring of the elderly victim.[1]

DILEMMAS IN ELDER ABUSE

While there are similarities between elder abuse and other forms of family violence, there are some dilemmas unique to elder abuse. - Like many other victims of family violence, abused elders are dependent on the abusers for basic survival needs. However, the battered elderly parents also bear the additional stigma and guilt of having raised a child who mistreats them, and risk further harm if they seek help to alleviate the violence. This makes them ashamed and afraid to ask for help.

- The overwhelming majority of caretakers are women, and they also comprise the majority of vulnerable elderly. Women, then, face double jeopardy; they bear the stresses and strains of caring for an elderly woman and they face a high probability of later being in a similar situation.[2,3] One care giver, a sixty-four-year-old married woman, blamed her estrangement from her husband and daughter on her having to care for her demanding ninty-two-year-old mother who lived with them. She said, " . . . and my family has just had it, they've abandoned me." This woman noted later that her mother would not contribute to household expenses. "I'm looking after her and I could be getting paid for what I do. She doesn't feel that way about it. I'm her daughter and she feels it's my obligation to care for her."

- A double-bind factor is faced by care givers who are caring for still older dependent kin. The average age of the dependent elderly is just over eighty and their ages range from sixty to ninety-nine.

The average age of care-giving children is forty-eight, with a range of 23 to 65 years. Thus the aging caretakers, in addition to facing retirement, fixed incomes, and increased health problems, bear the responsibility for a still older parent or family member. The effect of this additional burden on "older" care givers is reflected in a comment made by a sixty-year-old daughter with regard to her eighty-six-year-old father:

I don't consider him to be a burden. I'd be glad to be able to always take care of him if he wasn't so unpredictable, and I could. I know it sounds selfish, but I'm not getting any younger, and I want to do something for myself.

- A fourth dilemma is the double direction of the nature of the violence. While violence perpetrated on elders by their adult children has been publicized and sensationalized in the media, violence by elders on their middle-aged children has remained unnoticed. The authoritarian father who ruled his wife and children with an iron fist and met a loss of authority or control by beating them apparently can still resort to these techniques at eighty, especially when he finds controlling "the children" more difficult. One daughter in her fifties was unable to get out to do her own errands because her father felt it was her place to remain home and respond to his demands. When she would leave, he would violently attack any caretakers left with him and turn his room into a shambles.

- The final dilemma is that of the double demands which result when the care givers find themselves caught between two or more generations. At the very time that one's own family income is leveling off, this middle generation often has to assume the costs of caretaking for parents, and may still be responsible for younger or young-adult children. The value system is then strained. Who takes priority? The parents who raised them, or their own children, who may not yet be fully independent? Caught in such a dilemma, the middle generation often finds that they have limited physical, psychic, and financial cushions—if any at all.[4]

CAUSES OF ELDER ABUSE

Much that has been offered as theoretical work on elder abuse involves theories that have been developed and applied to other forms of intrafamily abuse.[5] Giordano and Giordano[6] present hypotheses related to several theories about the factors that lead to elder abuse. Many of these overlap and it is likely that abuse is triggered by the interplay of several of these factors.

Family Dynamics

A major premise is that violence is a normative behavioral pattern which is learned in the context of the family. That is, children learn from observing and participating in the family that violence is an acceptable response to stress; they may even learn a variety of responses for future behavior.[7]

Impairment and Dependence

The most likely people to be abused are women with severe physical or mental impairment.[8,9] According to O'Rourke,[10] such impairments lead to dependence which makes the person vulnerable to abuse. A corollary to the hypothesis of dependence owing to impairments is the concept of learned helplessness. According to this concept, elderly people may come to feel as they become increasingly dependent that they have no control over their lives and that they can do nothing to change their situation.[11]

Personality Traits of the Abuser

The abuser has traits that cause him or her to be abusive. While researchers consider this explanation too simplistic, personality traits are still a factor to be considered,[12] a related hypothesis being that adult children are abusive because of an abnormal childhood that did not foster their ability to make appropriate judgments.[13]

Filial Crises

Several theorists[14] have suggested that elder abuse may be the result of the failure of an adult child to resolve the filial crisis. According to this hypothesis, a task of adult children, in developing, is to go beyond the stage of adolescent rebellion toward emancipation from their parents. Often parent-child conflicts that are generated in adolescence continue into later life.[15]

Internal Stress

The responsibility of caring for a dependent, aged relative can lead to a stressful situation for the family which can lead to abuse.[16] O'Rourke[17] found that care givers spent an average of 24 hours a week providing physical and psychological assistance to frail aged relatives. Two-thirds of the care givers in his study reported

they were exhausted and anxious and that their health had
deteriorated.

External Stress

In the 1970s research on family violence recognized that external
stress on the family is the major factor that contributes to violence.
Straus, Gelles, and Steinmetz[18] found that important correlates of
domestic violence are age, income level, and employment status.
Block and Sinott[19] considered the presence of economic stress to
be one way in which elder abuse resembles other types of domestic
violence.

Negative Attitudes Toward the Aged

Patterns of elder abuse may be reinforced by the negative
stereotypes of elderly persons and their roles in society. Block and
Sinnott[20] and Kalish[21] point out that expectations may distort
perceptions. The resulting misperceptions may be a force in
situations occurring that are conducive to abuse because these
negative attitudes tend to dehumanize elderly persons and make
it easier for an abuser to victimize them without feeling remorse.

RECOGNIZING ABUSE

Recognizing and defining what constitutes abuse may be
difficult. It involves the use of clinical social work skills in observing
behaviors and interactions between the generations, in interviewing
all the members of the client system, and in making a diagnostic
assessment based on this information. Abuse can take a number
of different forms. The following categories of elder abuse were
cited by the Select Committee on Aging (1981):
- *Physical Abuse*: Violence that results in bodily harm or
  mental distress. It includes assault, unjustified denial of one's
  rights, sexual abuse, restrictions on freedom of movement,
  and murder.
- *Negligence*: A breach of duty or carelessness that results in
  injury or the violation of rights.

- *Financial Exploitation*: Theft or conversion of money or objects of value belonging to an elderly person by a relative or caretaker, through force or through misrepresentation.
- *Psychological Abuse*: The provoking of the fear of violence or isolation, including name calling and other forms of verbal assault and threats. It can be spontaneous or a planned effort to dehumanize.
- *Violation of Rights*: The breaching of rights that are guaranteed to all citizens by the Constitution, federal, and state statutes.

SOCIAL WORK INTERVENTIONS

Caseworkers have different resources and intervention strategies available in their community that can be employed to ameliorate problems of elder abuse and neglect. A major step working with, as well as preventing, cases of abuse would be to acknowledge the family's contribution to the care of the elderly person and to provide services that support and enhance the care-giving role.

- How complete is the caregiver's knowledge of the client's medical condition? Are the expectations of the elder person realistic? What difficulties is the caretaker experiencing in caring for or living with the patient? What other responsibilities does the caretaker have at home or on the job? What support systems are available for the care giver? Is he or she able to support a dependent elderly relative? Ask the caregiver to describe a typical day.
- Danger signs are abnormal behavior during the interview— hostility, exhibiting too little or too much concern for the patient's problems. A high-risk situation exists when the care giver is dependent on the patient for housing and money or has been forced by circumstances to care for the family member but does not really want to.
- Asking direct questions related to abuse may be a touchy matter. The caseworker may start out by saying "Have you ever felt so frustrated with your dad that you. . . .?" or, "It's very hard dealing with a person who is confused and loud, do you ever medicate him when you go out to shop?" Giving the care giver the benefit of the doubt, work with him or her to rule out, directly or indirectly,

hitting, shaking, verbal threats, withholding food, and slapping. If the care giver has power of attorney or has joint accounts with the patient, try to rule out misuse of money or property.

- The necessity for being specific but tactful in questioning about the possibility of abuse with the elder patient cannot be overemphasized. Many an inexperienced caseworker has been misled about the seriousness of aggressive behavior because he did not inquire about the details of the phenomenology of the act. Knowing an adult son has a "temper problem" is not enough. The worker will want to inquire about the frequency, type, and duration of the violent acts or threats. In particular, one wants to elicit information about the target for the violence, e.g., people or furniture. Did the son slap his mother or hit her with his fist? Was this done in anger, or was the son in control of his temper at the time? Assumptions should not be made that the violent acts are only the result of a disturbed psyche or family system, as organic contributions to violence are numerous.

- The caseworker should be careful, too, not to probe too quickly or deeply if an initial family conjoint interview is held, as an argument may ensue which could have several unfortunate consequences—turning the family off to the idea of treatment, or impelling the adult child to walk out of the interview or become aggressive.

- When treating these cases, the caseworker should try to get the elder patient to agree on a plan on how to react if there is a future violent episode. Some parents find it impossible to call the police even if there has been life-threatening violence. Most often one parent will agree to do this while the other parent refuses on the grounds it's too harsh, too sensational, etc. Often the adult child and the parent will make elaborate rationalizations for the violent behavior. The child then colludes with the other parent in explaining his actions as justifiable. The parent may say the adult child was under stress, drunk, etc., using these explanations as an excuse for the violent behavior and thereby sanctioning the lack of corrective action.

When the caseworker hears this, it is crucial that he confront this attitude. The family can be told that there is *no* excuse for the violence, and that treatment and assistance should be established immediately. It is important that the caseworker not communicate any ambivalence about the aggressive actions, e.g., telling the family "Boys will be boys," as a way of explaining that they should not be too upset over the fact the son has hit his father. Sometimes this initial confrontation by a caseworker may be the one intervention that begins to change a long-standing pattern of intrafamilial abuse.

The assessment integrates patient history, care-giver history, and results of the physical examination toward a diagnosis of:
- no evidence of elder abuse/neglect
- suspicion of elder abuse/neglect
- positive evidence of abuse/neglect

If the caseworker suspects violence may be at the root of injuries, his management must include, in addition to investigation and treatment of all injuries, the following steps:

- Determination of the immediate danger for the victim and any other family members;

- Admission into the hospital or to community shelter for the victim;

- Documentation of the events described, as this is useful now and may be of value should future incidents point to abuse. Some states now require mandatory reporting of elder abuse; procedures are similar to mandatory reporting for child abuse.

- Do not neglect the adult child who needs an opportunity for an objective evaluation, as well as an opportunity to reduce the stress of maladaptive functioning. They require as much assistance as the elder victim. Thus, support groups, mental health services, and family life education programs that are directed toward helping families understand the aging process and the unique circumstances of the adult child are needed.

- "Respite care" for the parent should be investigated to give the care giver a break, and adult day care is another excellent short-term solution, as is gaining financial and medical insurance eligibility in order to ease the burden of care.

- Assisting the patient and family with chore-services, meals-on-wheels, visiting nurses, and home health aides is vital.

- Other linkages that can stop abuse include: family counseling to defuse conflicts; assertiveness training for the victim; educating the care giver on appropriate care (e.g., brochures on Alzheimer's and related diseases); home improvements, such as ramps or rails to make the elder person less dependent; education in self-care for the patient so as to reduce dependency; senior transportation to and from appointments.

- In some situations, the only remedy may be legal intervention in the form of guardianship proceeding or prosecution. Legal Aid and Protective Services Organizations are important resources. Mandatory laws make the legal intervention easier and remove the burden of prosecution from the abused person and the institution involved.

CONCLUSION

The complexities of coordinating the delivery of services are compounded by the nature of elder abuse which sometimes requires an emergency response and heightens issues of professional ethics and confidentiality,[22] such as the need to substantiate the abuse while providing immediate services and maintaining confidentiality. The most appropriate approach would include coordinating the efforts of the various disciplines that provide essential supportive services. For example, the caseworker could function as case manager from point of entry to conclusion and ensure that health, legal, financial, and emergency services are provided when necessary. While these approaches are worthwhile, they may be difficult in terms of the cuts that have been made in social services. Any attempt, then, to effect impact on elder abuse necessitates that priorities be assigned. Therefore, the ultimate cost in relation to the anticipated benefit of all approaches will need to be reevaluated. Existing resources, such as access to computers, which have the capacity to dispense available data nationally and the pooling of information among agencies serving the aged can be used to lower the cost of such evaluations.[23]

Notes

1. Harbin, H. T. Violence against parents, *Medical Aspects of Human Sexuality*, Sept. 1983, Vol. 17, No. 9, pp. 20–42.
2. Steinmetz, S. K. Elder Abuse, *Aging*, Jan.–Feb. 1981, pp. 6–10.
3. Brody, E. Women's changing role, the aging family and long-term care of older people, *National Journal*, Oct. 1979, Vol. 11, pp. 1823–33.
4. Steinmetz, S. *Elder abuse: The hidden problem.* Prepared statement, Briefing by the Select Committee on Aging, U. S. House of Representatives, Boston, MA, June 23, 1979. Washington, D. C., 1980, pp. 7–10.
5. Pedrick-Cornell, C. & Gelles, R. Elderly abuse: The status of current knowledge, *Family Relations*, July 1982, *31*, pp. 457–65.
6. Giordano, N. & Giordano, J. Elder abuse: A review of the literature, *Social Work*, May–June 1984, pp. 232–36.
7. Lau, E. & Kosberg, J. Abuse of the elderly by informal care-providers: Practice and research issues, Paper presented at the 31st Annual Meeting of the Gerontological Society, Dallas, TX, November 20, 1978.
8. Block, M. & Sinnott, J. (Eds.). *The battered elder syndrome, an exploratory study.* Unpublished manuscript. University of Maryland Center on Aging, 1979.
9. Burson, G. R. Granny-battering, *British Medical Journal*, September 6, 1975, Vol. 3, p. 562.
10. O'Rourke, M. *Elder abuse: The state of the art*, Paper prepared for the National Conference on the Abuse of Older Persons. Boston, MA: March 2-25, 1981.
11. Davidson, J., Hennessy, S. & Sledge, S. Additional factors related to elder abuse, In Block & Sinnott (Eds.), *The battered elder syndrome*.
12. O'Rourke, M. *Elder abuse: The state of the art*.
13. Ibid.
14. Block, M. & Sinnott, J. *The battered elder syndrome*, and Lau & Kosberg, *Abuse of the elderly by informal Careproviders: Practice and research issues.*
15. Farrar, M. Mother and daughter conflicts extended into later life. In *Social Casework*, May 1955, *36*, pp. 202–07.
16. Block & Sinnott, *The battered elder syndrome*.

17. O'Rourke, M. *Elder abuse: The state of the art.*
18. Steinmetz, S., Straus, M., & Gelles, R. *Behind closed doors: Violence in the American family.* New York: Anchor Press/Doubleday, 1980.
19. Block & Sinnott, The battered elder syndrome.
20. Ibid.
21. Kalish, R. The new ageism and the failure models: A polemic. *The Gerontologist*, Aug. 1979, *19*, pp. 398–402.
22. O'Rourke, M. *Elder abuse: The state of the art.*
23. Giordano, N. H. & Giordano, J. *Elder abuse: A review of the literature.*

Chapter 8

THE RAPE VICTIM

Barbara Moynihan

IMPLICATIONS FOR SOCIAL WORK PRACTICE

Social workers have historically been viewed as supporters and advocates for those who seek their services. The need for this intervention is magnified in the case of the victim of rape. Treatment of the rape victim continues to be judgmental, incomplete, and often episodic.

Rape represents the ultimate of sexist values and attitudes.[1] Most victims of rape are women and most first responders (medical and police) are male, thus reinforcing the biases that women are still confronted by in a patriarchal society.

Why rape continues to occur and, in fact, to increase in frequency,[2] can be understood if one reviews the history that has perpetuated women as acceptable and even appropriate victims of violence.

The Bible has told us that women are responsible for all of the trouble in the world. When God confronted Adam in the Garden of Eden and accused him of eating the forbidden fruit—Adam's excuse was, "the woman whom thou gavest to be with me, she gave me the fruit of the tree and I ate."[3] An old Hebrew tradition holds that God's first creation included a female child called Lillith, the first defender of the cause of women's liberation. When Adam told Lillith that she was to obey his wishes, she replied: "We are equal, we are made of the same earth."[4] So saying, she flew into the air and transformed herself into a demon who ate children. Even that early in time, women who would not subjugate themselves to the will of men were seen as witches.[5]

Rape is often viewed as a symbol of the power relationship between the sexes: "Rape is to women as lynching was to blacks" — the ultimate physical threat by which all men keep all women in a state of psychological intimidation.[6]

It is always the woman who is raped. Rape is an aggressive act against *"women as woman"*.[7] The rapist is educated to his behavior by society. Rape is the extreme manifestation of approved activities in which one segment of society dominates another. Rape is a ritual of power.

"Rape was an insurrectionary act. It delighted me."[8]

Women are socialized to view themselves as sexual objects, subject to being acted upon by men. In our society, relations between the sexes are often viewed as an exchange, wherein female servility is seen as the price for male protection. The socialization process is such that women are educated to internalize the psychological characteristics of helpless victims who must rely on the protection of others.

Women learn the mythology of rape that ensures a male advantage and provides the rationale for perceiving herself as a legitimate victim for rape. She is taught that "nice girls do not get raped" and that she alone is responsible for avoiding the rape event.[9]

In dealing with victims of rape, the above references may provide a framework within which the social worker can begin to understand and address the verbal and nonverbal concerns and responses of the victim.

This chapter will deal primarily with the adult female victim of rape; however, it is important to note that men as well as children fall victim to this heinous act and that their comprehensive needs, although in some ways different, must also be addressed in a very specialized manner.

Rape has been defined in many ways: "the act of taking anything by force,"[10] "carnal knowledge of a person by force and against that person's will."[11] Rape is a crime of violence and aggression, and is perceived as, and often is, a life-threatening event. Rape encompasses a broad spectrum of experiences ranging from the surprise attack by a stranger, to insistence on sexual intercourse by an acquaintance or spouse.

Rape is one of the most unreported crimes in America. The FBI "estimates" that only one in 10 rapes is reported to the police. According to the 1984 Uniform Crime Report published by the FBI, there were more than 84,000 rapes reported in 1984. This represents a 7 percent increase over 1983 figures. College campuses are the location for a staggering number of "date" or acquaintance rapes that are, for the most part, not reported.[12] It is estimated that one woman in three is at risk of being raped during her lifetime. This, coupled with gross underreporting, results in the assumption that an overwhelming number of women have been affected by rape either as children or as adults. An increased awareness by society, due in part to the women's movement, has resulted in appreciable improvement in services to rape victims. In conjunction with improved services, there is also an accompanying increase in the responsibilities of those professionals involved in both the immediate as well as the long-term treatment of this problem.

Rape victims who present themselves for care shortly after the crime has occurred often are presenting at a time of crisis. Crisis intervention techniques are essential. The profound difference in the sequelae of rape, as compared to other life-threatening crises, is that the victim's usual support system is more likely to be disrupted. The victim may experience an overwhelming sense of violation and helplessness which is a continuation of the powerlessness and intimidation experienced during the rape event.

Friends, families, and important others may alienate the victim due to their own biases and misperceptions of rape.

Once the victim comes forward seeking help, whether medical, legal, or social services, she becomes "public property."[13] *She at some level loses control over the events that follow disclosure.*

She is then at the mercy of public opinion, as well as of those providers involved with her care. Social work intervention is essential *as soon after disclosure as possible.* The social worker has a responsibility to maintain some knowledge of medical and evidence-gathering protocols, as well as a command knowledge regarding criminal justice procedures. In cases in which no criminal justice involvement is desired, the social worker must also provide support and reinforcement around the decision *not* to report.

Not only does the social worker have a responsibility to understand the impact, the implications, and the long-term effects of rape, but needs to identify the verbal and nonverbal messages communicated by the victim. The social worker needs to ask key questions and maintain a fund of knowledge sufficient to enable the clinician to really "listen," and to "hear" the answers. In rape cases, this is often hard for any social worker, male or female.

The goal in providing intervention to victims of sexual assault is to enable the client to return to a previous level of function, or to an improved pre-assault level of function. This, due in part to an identification of services and resources that may previously have been either unavailable or unknown to the client.

THE EFFECTS OF RAPE

"I thought I would die." "I could not believe that this was happening to me." Thus one young woman describes the emotional responses she experienced during her rape.

Sally S., a twenty-eight-year-old teacher, met a colleague at a regional conference. She agreed to dinner after the meeting and invited her companion to her apartment for a drink following dinner. She was sexually assaulted by this man in her apartment.

Sally sought medical attention from her physician but did not report the crime to the police because she was so embarrassed. She blamed herself. Sally went for therapy following a suicide attempt a month after the attack. She has since resigned her teaching position, moved from the area, and isolated herself from her friends and family. She describes feelings of fear, anxiety, and vulnerability. She never feels safe anymore. She experiences great anxiety around men and fears she will never feel self-confident again.

Rape is the ultimate violation of the self, an intrusion of the most personal kind, and often a life-threatening event. Rape is a crisis, a sudden, unexpected event that interrupts the victim's life. Much has been written about the impact of rape and particularly the psychological consequences of this experience. Most victims of rape do not require care directed at physical injuries. The most immediate need is for intervention directed toward the psychological impact of rape.

One needs to pay attention to the nature of the assault, the treatment of physical injuries when present, the relationship of the attacker to the victim, and the location of the attack. When the attack occurs in the home of the victim or when the attacker is someone known and trusted by the victim, the needs of the client are unique to issues around trust, ability to select companions, and safety at home, in addition to the myriad of additional psychological implications associated with the crisis of rape.

The practitioner must also be aware of the developmental issues involved in rape counseling. The intervention appropriate for an adolescent is quite different than that for the older adult whose concern is focused on an increased sense of morality and fragility, rather than the adolescent's concerns around independence and parental conflict. (See Table 1, adapted from Eric Erikson.)

Crisis intervention is the appropriate theoretical framework applicable in dealing with the emotional responses of a rape victim. This approach involves a brief, active, and focused intervention and has proven to be extremely effective. The social worker should involve the client in the interaction as quickly as possible in order to promote a sense of competency, control, and decision making. Due to the nature of rape and the powerlessness that accompanies the experience, active involvement by the victim is both an affirmation of competency and the beginning of recovery. The social worker or other clinician must be aware that although crisis intervention is time limited, usually 6 to 8 weeks, the trauma of rape is frequently exacerbated and symptoms often resurface beyond this time period. The victim should be referred to other agencies if problems continue.

The psychological responses to rape are very specific and unique to this experience and have been classified under the term Rape Trauma Syndrome. The rape event plunges the victim into a state of psychological disequilibrium. The aftermath of this experience results in feelings of intense fear, loss of control, and increased sense of vulnerability and some degree of impairment in thinking and decision making. Rape trauma syndrome refers to the acute phase and long-term reorganization process that occurs as a result of rape. This syndrome of behavioral, somatic, and psychological responses is an acute stress reaction to a life-threatening situation.

Rape trauma syndrome involves two phases. The first is experienced as a period of significant disorganization during which the client may have difficulty making decisions, may be extremely fearful, vigilant, and mistrustful. These feelings may be manifested in several fashions based on the client's previous coping strategies. Some clients may be very expressive, others very controlled and nonexpressive. Observable characteristics range from hysteria to anger, silence, or a flat, withdrawn presentation. Sleep and appetite disturbances are common during this phase; headaches, muscle fatigue, flashbacks, fear, guilt, and self-blame may also be experienced by the victim. Guilt and feelings of responsibility for the rape are factors which influence reporting the crime and seeking help from other systems. As an attempt at mastering and regaining control over her life, the victim may move, change her telephone number, leave school or work, and sometimes relocate to a geographical area distant from her present residence. Many victims experience phobic reactions following the trauma of rape. Some of the most common are fear of indoors, outdoors, crowds, sexual difficulty, and fear of being alone.

In some cases, there is either a current or past history of physical or psychological difficulties which are exacerbated as a result of the rape. In those cases it is advisable to work closely with the physician, agency, or therapist who knows or has treated the client. The social worker should be alert to the "silent reaction to rape." This reaction occurs when a victim of a previous undisclosed rape presents for care. In these cases the clinician may, through sensitive interviewing and an awareness of existing symptoms, enable the victim to work through unresolved issues associated with the previous attack.

As noted earlier, rape is one of the most unreported crimes. Some victims never seek treatment; thus the social worker who is alert to the "silent rape syndrome"[14] is key to the beginnings of healing for the client. Credibility and validation are critical factors in recovery. The victim of rape has experienced a significant trauma to her person, as well as to her sense of credibility, self-esteem, and integrity. The social worker plays a major role in facilitating the healing process in modeling appropriate modalities for other professionals. Follow-up care, beyond the initial contact, should be available to the client. Anniversary dates, court appearances, or a new crisis may trigger responses similar to those experienced in the immediate past rape period.

Support groups provide a valuable forum for reducing isolation and learning new strategies for coping with the aftermath and long-term effects of rape. Social workers should make referrals to community agencies if their agency does not have support group services.

Anticipatory guidance around predictable responses to rape greatly assists victims in coping with the neurovegetative signs, social, and physical aftermath of rape. Many victims describe an overwhelming sense of isolation and fear following the rape. The peer support group provides a therapeutic forum for reducing those feelings.

Acceptance, credibility, and power are critical factors in healing. It is important for the social worker to recognize when referrals to other agencies or therapists are indicated, because frequently the new crisis precipitates the emergence of old unresolved or repressed issues that the client now has the energy or interest to address.

Recent studies indicate that although resolution and reorganization occur within a reasonable time to most victims, there is indication that a significant number of rape victims report continuing symptoms many years after the assault.[15] For some victims, the rape event has resulted in positive changes; for example, they are more self-reliant, independent, and exhibit stronger behavior. However, for other victims, the changes are negative; fear, anxiety, depression, and changes in sexual attitudes and behavior are common. It is critical that the social worker maintain an awareness and understanding of the sequelae of rape that may continue well beyond the initial intervention and establish methods for the clients to recontact them or contact other long-term agencies.

As evidenced above, the issues and responses to rape are both complex and comprehensive. Rape affects almost every aspect of the victim's life, emotional, physical and social, and influences her future level of functioning as well.

The manner in which a victim is treated at the moment of disclosure has a profound effect on recovery. Thus, the victim whose request for help is responded to by skepticism and doubt may respond by withdrawing, and closing communications. Feelings of guilt and self-blame may be exaggerated, and significant long-term effects will almost predictably occur.

The goals in rape crisis intervention, restoring control and enabling the client to return to a pre-assault level of function or better, must be prominent in the mind of the clinician. Thus the social worker conducting the initial interview plays a major role in the future recovery of the client.

THE INITIAL INTERVIEW

Doreen S. is a twenty-five-year-old single medical student who was raped by a man who was hiding in her car. Following the attack, the rapist fled from the vehicle and Doreen was able to drive herself back to the hospital.

She was quite hysterical when she arrived but was able to regain her composure quickly and agreed to talk to the social worker and have the police department contacted. Doreen was quite relieved when the social worker arrived, and was verbal throughout the initial interview. She expressed concern about her ability to drive her car or feel safe in any motor vehicle again. She was also very concerned about the reaction of her boyfriend to her attack, since he had expressed concern for her safety on several previous occasions.

Doreen and the social worker made an appointment to meet with the boyfriend the next day to discuss the assault. Doreen agreed to having a physical examination and the collection of evidence for the police laboratory. She asked the social worker, a woman, to remain with her through this examination and while she was being interviewed by the police. She was anxious and upset. Many victims say it is like a second assault on their bodies.

The social worker encouraged Doreen to contact her family and close friends, for she needed their support. Her boyfriend would return the next day. A friend came to the hospital to drive Doreen home and agreed to stay with her for a few days. Prior to leaving the hospital, the social worker explained to Doreen and her friend the many responses that may follow such a sexual assault. She was warned to expect sleep and appetite disturbances, flashbacks, and generalized anxiety. This technique is called anticipatory guidance.

Follow-up intervention spanned a period of 8 weeks. This included several meetings with both Doreen and her boyfriend and one meeting with him alone. The social worker assisted with the criminal justice proceedings and offered continued support at the trial.

Doreen was advised of the significance of anniversary dates, and other long-term effects that she might experience. She was given the names of long-term services available plus the continued availability of the social worker. Doreen returned to her duties and responsibilities as a medical student; however, for a brief period of time, she did not drive her car alone and she parked in a different place. She occasionally experienced feelings of anxiety and fear. The support of her boyfriend and other friends and the continued availability of social work services seemed to enable her to resume her previous level of functioning within a reasonable period of time.

The client should be provided with privacy, an atmosphere which is low in sensory stimulation and an approach which fosters trust and open communications. The social worker who is uncomfortable or uninformed about the issues and impact of rape may have great difficulty in working with these clients. Knowledge of rape and the constellation of responses experienced by victims of rape is essential for effective intervention. Self-awareness on the part of the social worker is also essential.

The interview should be paced according to the client's ability to recount the details of the assault. The trauma of the attack may resurface as the interview proceeds. The client should be permitted to "take a break" or "time out" periodically. There may be some memory gaps, disorganization, or in some cases, an inability to continue the interview.

The crisis that the client has experienced and her responses to it will shape the initial interview as well as follow-up contacts. In cases in which the attack has recently occurred, it is of particular importance that the client be enabled to describe all of the details of the assault. The social worker should establish a climate of trust, credibility, and stability.

Active listening in a nonjudgmental atmosphere will enable the client to begin the process of recovery.

The client's ability to proceed is based not only on the interaction and response of the social worker, but is also influenced by the nature of the assault and the relationship of the attacker to the victim, as well as her previous history. It is important to note that although some clients will seek help immediately after the assault, not all do. Thus, disclosure of rape may occur months or years after the attack. Resolution begins with disclosure. The trauma once discussed can also result in heightened feelings of anxiety and vulnerability. The informed social worker will be attuned to these responses and to the need for frequent contact with the client. It is not unusual in cases that involve delayed disclosure for acute crisis symptomatology to be observed. Sleep and appetite disturbances as well as extreme feelings of insecurity often are seen in cases of this nature. *Repressed feelings, once communicated, no longer require energy to contain; thus the client may experience a feeling of tremendous loss and confusion.*

The social worker should monitor suicidal ideation, as well as the client's level of function. These as well as the mental status exam are key factors in assessing the client's current status, as well as in planning future interventions. The importance of the initial interview cannot be overemphasized. The myriad of issues that surface as a result of rape begin to be identified and addressed with the first contact.

The goal of the clinician is to enable the client to recall the stress with assimilation and affective sharing of the experience and eventual recovery.

There is no simplistic approach to the management of the rape victim and her family/significant other; however, initial intervention by a sensitive and informed practitioner has a major influence on resolution and recovery.

THE SIGNIFICANT OTHER

Dealing with families and "important others" is an integral part of social work intervention. When the issue involves rape, the intervention must address responses that are very similar to those expressed by the victim. Feelings of guilt, helplessness, anger, and powerlessness are all often experienced by the significant other, who may also feel a distorted sense of failure to protect the victim. These feelings, if not dealt with by the social worker, will influence the ability of the family or significant other to support the victim. Families and important others should be viewed as "secondary victims."[16] A forum should be afforded them within which their feelings and concerns may be addressed. The presence of a support system is a key factor in recovery. The professional who excludes the family or significant other from the "therapeutic relationship" may reinforce biases about rape as well as about its victims and inhibit or delay the recovery of the victim. Facilitation through medical, legal, and other systems is much smoother when an "important other" is included. Each case is unique, and although there are general guidelines which assist in the treatment plan, the worker needs to be acutely aware of the special characteristics of each case. Ethnic and cultural differences, the age of the victim, the meaning of the event to both the victim and family, as well as the previous status of the relationship, will direct the focus for the social worker.

This information can only be obtained through careful interviewing and history-taking by the clinician who has special skills in rape crisis intervention. Children of clients are of major concern, not only as additional responsibilities of the victim but also as "secondary victims." The ages of the children and perception of the attack as well as the family history will direct the work of the social worker with the children of the victim. There are times when the child feels responsible for the attack, particularly if there has been conflict within the family. This results in a tremendous sense of guilt. At times the child perceives his/her role as protector of the parent—obviously unrealistic, and another indicator for intervention. The social worker should carefully assess each situation, anticipate needs and enable the victim and significant others to plan effective coping strategies. Not all victims will be members of an intact family or be involved in a positive relationship, so the initial support system may consist of only the social worker. Exploring other resources with the victim is extremely important. Referral and resource utilization is often helpful.

Rape Crisis Services, Women's Centers and other agencies may offer services and support groups that may bridge the gap for the isolated client. Generalizations and stereotypes are obviously inappropriate in the human services field since they tend to result in the exclusion of some clients from appropriate and necessary services. In the treatment of rape victims and their significant others, a nonjudgmental approach is critical to open communications, trust, and credibility. It is not unusual for clinicians to approach their clients using a heterosexual frame of reference, thus blocking communications with the homosexual client and his/her significant other.

Offering to notify an "important other" can be articulated in a very general manner, i.e., "Is there someone you would like me to call," versus "Would you like me to notify your husband or boyfriend," which inhibits the lesbian victim from openly discussing her fears and concerns not only about her responses to the assault but those of her important other as well.

There are many considerations involved in working with families and important others. Racial and cultural differences, age and developmental stage of the victim, as well as the status of the relationship within the family system will be predictors of the degree of support possible from the family system. There may be times when it will be appropriate to work individually with the members of the support system. This service should be offered and continued for as long as indicated. The social worker should also consider other resources which may be utilized for referral for long-term intervention when indicated. The new crisis (the assault) may result in unresolved issues being raised not only in the victim but in the family as well. Reassurance and a forum for discussion will enable the family/significant other to address their own responses and needs and provide the support so necessary to the victim as she moves toward recovery.[17]

MEDICAL AND FORENSIC IMPLICATIONS

Although the social worker is not expected to be an expert on either the medical or legal aspects of sexual assault, some knowledge is necessary in order to reassure and support the client through either or both of these systems.

Medical care should address:

1.   treatment of any physical injuries or preexisting disease which has been exacerbated due to the trauma of the attack;
2.   prevention of venereal disease;

3. prevention of pregnancy;
4. careful forensic examination and evidence collection when indicated;
5. acknowledgment and treatment to address the psychological sequelae of rape.

Many hospitals have formal protocols which very clearly outline all procedures to be followed in the treatment and management of sexual assault victims. These documents should be familiar to the social worker who may be asked to testify in court when police and criminal justice systems are involved. Social worker records may also be subpoenaed. Careful nonjudgmental documentation is critical to the credibility of the victim and the successful outcome of the case. (Chapter 3 outlines this in more detail.)

The social worker has a dual role in the case of the sexual assault victim, primarily as the therapist whose work with the client will result in a return to a pre-assault level of function. The second role is to simplify and facilitate the medical examination, the police interview and statement and, ultimately, the court process. Continuity and open communications are important factors in sexual assault cases. Continuity is not always possible in the criminal justice system; thus the importance of consulting with a rape crisis worker and a rape crisis service police/court advocate to bridge the gap. Many victims feel that if contact from the police is episodic or has stopped, their case is no longer important. Constant reassurance and sharing of information will alleviate these concerns and result in follow-through by the client. Consultation by the social worker with experts in the field will greatly assist in the management of the sexual assault victim. Rape crisis counselors receive extensive and focused training on all aspects of rape. Their value as consultants and facilitators is unquestioned. A multidisciplinary approach is most appropriate and successful in dealing with the client who has been sexually assaulted.

THE STATE OF THE ART IN RAPE CRISIS SERVICES

Although there have been significant strides and improvements in the treatment of rape victims, there are still gaps in services that have impact on the victim, family, and society at large. Legislation directed at mandated training for police officers in rape crisis intervention, as well as funding for rape crisis services, are major advances in this field. Spousal rape can now be prosecuted in many of the states. The complex issues for the victim and family in cases of spousal rape can now be addressed in a more focused manner. The legitimizing of the woman's right to say no to her husband's demands for sexual intercourse represents a major advance in rape crisis work.

The growth and comprehensiveness of community-based rape crisis services has provided a valuable resource for victims and professionals. The elimination of rape is contingent on education, sensitization, and legislation. Innovative and comprehensive services to victims can be developed only when society recognizes the meaning of this crime, how and why it is perpetuated, and the context in which it occurs.

Rape will be eliminated only through intense reworking of social values and standards and a reorientation of the relationships and roles between the sexes.

Treatment for offenders, juvenile as well as adult, does not exist in any consistent fashion. Incarceration and episodic attempts at treatment have not had significant impact on the frequency of the crime.

Early detection of potential offenders as well as appropriate services to address this population are still to be developed.

Professionals who enter the human services field often have little or no information regarding rape, battering, or violence in the family. Until comprehensive curricula are integrated into the education of physicians, nurses, social workers, and other providers, the gaps in services will continue to exist.

The social worker who is unable to ask the "key" questions, the medical practitioner who understands the physical and nonverbal signs of abuse, and the therapist who is aware of the long-term impact of violence, can all effect change, healing, and a change in the "status quo."

It is hoped that this text will generate a new level of interest and intervention in the treatment of victims of rape, as well as all forms of violence in the family.

Table 7-1.

Concerns of Victims

Age	
Infant–3 years	1. Infant's trust in adults 2. Inhibition of autonomy
Age 4–7	1. Area of body selected as the focus of attack 2. Sex in terms of difference in genitalia will also register
Age 8–10	1. Issue of rape can be blurred with physical development 2. Knowledge and understanding of the part of the body involved and the connection with sex
Age 13–19	1. Difficulty in talking about the rape, especially to adults 2. Confronted with the issue of sexuality 3. Possibility of pregnancy
Young Adult	1. Telling people about the attack, i.e., boyfriend, spouse 2. Pregnancy issue 3. Disease issue
Adulthood	1. How this will affect others 2. How this will affect life-style 3. Concerns that victim might transmit a disease to children 4. Possibility of pregnancy 5. How to tell family and how will they react
Older Adult	1. Sexual assault not primary focus 2. Sensitive to the fear of death 3. More trauma noted in older women 4. Sexual issue, i.e., society has ambivalent attitudes about older people and their sexual activity

[18]Adapted from E. Erickson's Stages of Development

Notes

1. Brownmiller, S. *Against our will: Men, women and rape.* New York: Simon & Schuster, 1975.
2. *FBI Uniform Crime Report*, 1984.
3. Genesis 3:11.
4. Genesis 3:12.
5. Hays, H. R. *The dangerous sex: The myth of feminine evil.* New York: Putnam, 1964, p. 144.
6. Brownmiller, S. *Against our will: Men, women and rape.*
7. Metzger, D. It is always the woman who is raped. *American Journal of Psychiatry*, April 1976, *133*:4, 405–408. American Psychiatric Association, Washington, D.C.
8. Cleaver, E. *Soul on ice*, 1962. McGraw, New York.
9. Weis, K., & Borgs, S. S. Victimology and rape: The case of the legitimate victim. *Issues in Criminology* Fall 1973, *8*:2, 71–115. Crime and Social Justice Association, San Francisco.
10. *Oxford English Dictionary*, 1971 edition.
11. Evrarp, S. Rape: The medical, social and legal implications. *American Journal of Obstetrics & Gynecology* 1971, *111*:2, 197–199, C. V. Mosby Co. St. Louis.
12. Schieltz, L. G., & DeSavage, J. *Rape and rape attitudes on a college campus.* Journal of Victimology, 1975. National Institute of Victimology, Arlington, VA.
13. Hilberman, E. *The rape victim.* American Psychiatric Society, 1976. Garamond/Pridemark Press, Inc., Baltimore, Maryland.
14. Burgess, A. W., & Holmstrom, L. L. Rape trauma syndrome. *American Journal of Psychiatry.* 131:9, 981–86, September 1974. American Psychiatric Assoc. Washington, D.C.
15. Lifton, J. The survivor syndrome. *Death in life, Survivors of Hiroshima.* New York; Random House, 1967.
15. Nadelson, C. C., Notman, M., Zackson, H., Crornick, J. *The long-term impact of rape: A follow-up study*, Paper presented at Harvard Science Center, May 1980.
17. Hoff, L. A., & Williams, T. Counseling the rape victim and her family. *Crisis Intervention* 6(4), pp. 2–13, 1975. Human Sciences Press, New York.
18. Erikson, E. *Childhood and society.* New York: Norton, 1964. (Table 1).

Chapter 9

PORNOGRAPHY AND ITS
RELATION TO VIOLENCE

Donna Waldron DiGioia

Pornography is a systematic practice of exploitation and
subordination based on sex which differentially harms
women . . . The bigotry and contempt it promotes, with the
acts of aggression it fosters, diminish opportunities for equality
of rights . . . create public and private harassment, persecution
and denigration; promote injury and degradation such as rape,
battery and prostitution and inhibit just enforcement of laws
against these acts.[1]

THE BIG BUSINESS OF DEGRADING WOMEN

With the advent of cable pay television, the availability of video
movie rental shops, and the corresponding increase in usage of
videocassette recorders, and the proliferation of mail-order vendors
marketing sexually explicit materials, there is an abundance of
pornographic material entering the American home. Many people
have expressed concern about the impact of this material on women,
children, and the family as a unit.

Pornography is a booming business. Currently it is an $8
billion-a-year industry in the U.S. alone, up from $7 billion in
1983 [2] There are more than 165 monthly "male" magazines bought

regularly by 18 million men.[3] In 1980, there were three to four times as many adult bookstores as McDonald's.[4] *Playboy* and *Penthouse* alone have a combined readership of 24 million.[5] The "adult" movie industry draws 3 million viewers a week. In 1978 it grossed $365 million. Today, of course, it is not necessary to leave home to see a pornographic film. In 1983 an estimated 2 million American households subscribed to cable television services featuring pornography.[6] Additionally, of the 14,000 video stores nationwide, 75 percent sell pornographic cassettes, which account for 50 to 60 percent of all prerecorded cassette sales.

Technology has led to bizarre trends such as video-game cartridges like *Custer's Revenge*, (featuring rape) *Beat 'Em and Eat 'Em*, (featuring the sexual abuse of prostitutes), and *Bachelor Party* (also featuring rape). In January 1985, *SexTex*, a computer system, was offered which includes shop-at-home service that allows you to sell and offer XXX merchandise. Pornographers have not stopped at visual images either; *High Society Magazine's* service (Dial-a-Porn) receives an estimated 500,000 telephone calls daily.[7] Even with the volume of this material, some are still unclear as to how pornography is defined. Additionally, all do not agree on a definition.

The 1971 Commission on Obscenity and Pornography defined pornography as the "verbal or pictorial explicit representations of sexual behavior that have as a distinguishing characteristic 'the degradation and demeaning portrayal of the role and status of the human female . . . as a mere sexual object to be exploited and manipulated sexually'."[8] Etymology provides another definition; pornography has its roots in the words *porne* and *graphos*, which together mean "writing about whores." *Porne* means whore or female captive which in ancient Greece was a woman available to all male citizens for their use and abuse. She was clearly a sexual slave afforded no protection. She was held in contempt. "Contemporary pornography conforms to the root meaning: the graphic depiction of vile whores, or in our language, sluts, cows (as in: sexual cattle, sexual chattel), cunts. The only change in the meaning of the word is with respect to its second part, *graphos*: now there are cameras—there is still photography, film, video."[9] Technology demands that real women be tied up, beaten, raped, and whipped, not merely written about. In this context, women exist only to serve male needs to dominate and sexually use them. Women's bodies are objectified in all forms of pornography; that is, women are depicted as objects whose sole justification for existence is the sexual pleasure of the (usually) male viewer. The more violent forms of pornography common today depict women and/or children being violently abused and degraded. Such images include rape, bondage, torture, physical and psychological brutality, sexual exploitation and, in some cases, murder, all for the purpose of the sexual stimulation of its male participants and male viewers. Although people sometimes disagree with a unified definition of pornography, and often disagree with a solution, there is growing acknowledgment that the drastic increase in the production, distribution, and consumption of pornography is cause for grave concern. The newer wave of sadistic pornography is cause for alarm. The fusion of sexuality with violence and degradation of females (and children) has harmful effects upon all of society and exacerbating effects upon the victimization of women. By associating male sexual arousal with brutality against women, women become real or potential victims of violent crimes, particularly violent crimes of a sexual nature.

> Even when they (pornographic films) do not overly depict scenes of violence and degradation of women at the hands of men, such as rape, beatings, and subordination, the tone is consistently anti-feminist, with women only serving to act as sexual slaves to men, being made use of, and ultimately being deprived of their right to a sexual climax. In the majority of such films, the portrayal ends with the men spraying their semen over the faces and breasts of the women.[10]
>
> Does one need scientific methodology in order to conclude that the anti-female propaganda that permeates our nation's cultural output promotes a climate in which acts of sexual hostility directed against women are not only tolerated but ideologically encouraged?[11]
>
> The pattern rarely changes in the porn culture. After a few preliminary skirmishes women invite or demand further violation, begging male masters to rape them into submission,

torture, and violence. In this fantasy land, females wallow in physical abuse and degradation. It is a pattern of horror which we have seen in our examination of sex cases translated again and again into actual assaults. . . .[12]

Explicit violence has been steadily increasing in recent years. In one 3-month period, a group of researchers viewed 26 porn films in San Francisco. Of these, 21 had rape scenes, 16 had bondage and torture scenes, two had films of child molestation, and two featured the killing of women for sexual stimulation.[13] Blatantly violent magazines usually found only in porn shops cost anywhere from $5 to $15. However, one does not have to frequent porn shops to obtain a magazine exhibiting such violence. A magazine called *Bondage* depicts women being tied up, and scissors, hot irons, torches, and knives held to their breasts and vaginas.[14] *Hustler* magazine has featured a cover story called *Women Under the Gun*, in which a gun was shown pointed at the woman's head on the cover; in the centerfold, in separate photos, it was pointed at her breasts, vagina, and buttocks. This publication has also depicted gang rape, a nude woman being pushed through a meat grinder, and a woman hunted down, captured, spread-eagled and tied up, by two (male) hunters.

Another magazine, *Brutal Trio*, depict three men who kidnap a woman, a twelve-year-old girl, and a grandmother, beat them and kick them in the face, body, and head. After the victims pass out, they are raped and beaten again. *Columbine Cuts Up*, a feature in an issue of *Chic* magazine, portrays a young woman thrusting a large knife into her vagina with blood spurting out from the wound. These magazines can be found in neighborhood newsstands.

Other gruesome scenes depicted in magazines and films are women being gagged, bound, and hung upside down, hot wax dripping on their breasts, or a woman's nipple being teased raw with a pliers. Titles of typical films are self-explanatory: *Angels of Pain, Sex and Rape, Beat the Bitch, Three Raped Virgins,* or *See Him Tear and Kill Her.* Films depicting incestuous themes and child abuse are *Daddy's Little Girls, Little Paula and Uncle Jake,* or *Justine: A Matter of Innocence.* The examples are endless, beyond imagination, and very difficult, at best, to confront.

In March of 1983 a twenty-one-year-old woman was gang-raped on a pool table in a local New Bedford, Massachusetts bar as the other patrons cheered. Was it a mere coincidence that shortly before the attack a local porno theater ran a film showing a woman having sex on a pool table? Additionally, 2 months prior to the rape, the January issue of *Hustler* magazine featured a photo layout of a woman being wrestled to a pool table, stripped, and raped by four men.

In December 1985, *Penthouse* magazine featured a photo layout of bound and tortured Asian women hung in trees. They appear to be unconscious or dead. One month later in January 1986 an eight-year-old Asian girl was kidnapped, raped, murdered, and hung nude from a tree limb. One can only speculate as to the possible connection between the photo images and these incidences. In April 1984, a 9-year-old boy was convicted of first-degree murder for the torture death of an eight-month-old baby girl. The boy and his brother testified that in sexually abusing the baby with a pencil and coat hanger, they were mimicking acts in pornography magazines they saw in their house. Their mother acknowledged that she kept pornography magazines in full view.[15]

More highly publicized examples of individuals imitating what the media depicts are John Hinckley, Jr.'s emulation of the central character in the film *Taxi Driver* when he shot President Reagan, and then of sexual molestation of a nine-year-old girl with a bottle by a group of other girls after they supposedly watched a similar assault in a TV movie called *Born Innocent*.

These examples are the most obvious and most publicized; however, it is important to keep in mind that pornography seems to affect many women's personal lives in some way. In 1978, a study of 929 women asked the question: "Have you ever been upset by anyone trying to get you to do what they'd seen in pornographic pictures, movies, or books?" Eight-nine (10 percent) said yes, they had been upset by such an experience *at least* once.[16] Research has shown that areas with a heavy concentration of pornography have higher rates of rape. Indeed, 44 percent of all women have been victims of rape or attempted rape, 38 percent of little girls are sexually molested inside and outside the home and, in one random sample study, only 7.8 percent of the women surveyed had *not* been sexually assaulted.[17] These statistics are alarming and should cause people to demand reasons for this amount of sexual violence against women and children.

Pornography has become such a pervasive and invasive force in our lives that even those who do not purposely seek pornography are exposed on an almost daily basis. Buying a newspaper at a local newsstand, a quart of milk at the corner store, looking through the local newspaper, driving down the street while signs advertising "Nude Girls" flash in your face, or even flipping on your own television set are all occasions where pornographic images have the opportunity to invade the conscious mind. It becomes all too clear that we are indeed living in a porn-culture, that is, a society in which pornography, even violent pornography, is so deeply entrenched in every facet of people's daily lives that it has become not only acceptable, but the norm.

CAUSE AND EFFECT

The proliferation of pornography has caused a renewed interest on the part of the Commission on Pornography, which released their current findings in late June 1986. The 1971 Presidential Commission on Obscenity and Pornography concluded that there was no evidence of a relationship between erotica and subsequent aggression, particularly sex crimes. Their verdict was that "all effects are trivial." These findings were later criticized for serious methodological and interpretational problems, and absence of distinction between erotic images and the violent pornography that is so common today.[18,19] The 1986 Commission took a much tougher stance. It called for a harsh crackdown on pornography through 92 recommendations, including both law enforcement and private action. The 1800 page report concluded that pornography contributes to assault, is defamatory and degrading, and constitutes a practice of sexual discrimination.[20]

In direct contradiction to the 1971 Commission on Pornography is the 1971 President's Commission on the Causes and Prevention of Violence. That Commission found that media violence can induce persons to act aggressively and suggested that media influence is probably long-lasting. According to the Commission on Violence:

> Violence on television encourages violent forms of behavior, and fosters moral and social values about daily life which are unacceptable in a civilized society.[21]

Leonard Berkowitz, Professor of Psychology at the University of Wisconsin, concludes:

> While our attitudes and ideologies dispose us to think that media sex can do no harm, research findings suggest to me that erotic materials may actually heighten the chances that a few persons will carry out the bizarre or deviant actions.[22]

In addition to the large body of evidence which points directly to the view that violence has very definite short-term effects and very probably long-term ones,[23] J. Phillippe Rushton demonstrated that television has the power to influence *prosocial* behavior. This conclusion is in accordance with the literature which suggests a relationship between television and antisocial behavior. The author believes that when antisocial and aggressive behavior are shown repeatedly and are uncontrolled, these behaviors not only become tolerable but become the norm. Rushton states:

> It is interesting to note that while television companies contend that their commercials can influence their audiences, they are not so eager to agree that their drama sequences can also affect viewer's conduct. The television companies cannot have it both ways. The message is quite clear: viewers learn from watching television and what they learn depends on what they watch.[24]

Evidence supporting feminist contentions evolved largely through research grounded in Social Learning Theory. In 1974, Victor Cline, a psychologist, edited a book on pornography entitled *Where Do You Draw the Line?* To demonstrate that classical and instrumental learning are relevant, he cites the work of S. Rachman of the Institute of Psychiatry in London who has done extensive research demonstrating that fetishism can be created in the laboratory.

> [He] exposed male subjects to colored photographic slides of nude females in sexually arousing positions along with a pair of female boots. Eventually, through simple conditioning, the male subjects were sexually aroused at merely seeing only a picture of the female boot.[25]

In pornography, sexual violence is most often coupled with arousal. Psychologist Seymour Feshbach believes that "the juxtaposition of violence with sexual excitement and satisfaction provides an unusual opportunity for the psychological conditioning of violent responses to erotic stimuli . . . when violence is fused with sex, we have a potentially dangerous form of alchemy."[26]

After an extensive review of the literature on media violence, Hans Eysenck and D. K. B. Nias conclude in their book *Sex, Violence and the Media*:

> It seems clear to us that there are certain areas of sexual behavior which should be completely excluded from the list of permitted activities (for depiction on film); sex involving children is one such area, rape and other forms of sexual violence, vividly and explicitly presented, are others. Sex involving animals would probably also come into this category . . . Torture, bondage and sadomasochistic acts involving sex may also be mentioned here. Such films may perhaps be shown on psychiatric prescription to patients addicted to such perversions, but they are not safe for public showing.[27]

They further believe:

> Where the context is hostile to women, as most pornographic films are, we feel that such films should fall under the category of "incitement to violence towards minority groups"—even though women are not a minority group. Nevertheless such films do constitute a clear case of incitement to maltreat

women, downgrade them to a lower status, regard them as mere sex objects, and elevate male machismo to a superior scale of values. Evaluative conditioning, modeling, and desensitization all point to the same conclusion, namely that such presentations have effects on men's attitudes which are detrimental to women; in fairness to more than one half of of population, such incitements would be proscribed.[28]

In his book *Psychology Is About People*, Professor Eysenck says that exposure to depictions of violence are conditioned, not on the grounds of immediate mimetic behavior, but by desensitization by gradual exposure in much the same way that phobic patients are desensitized to anxiety-producing stimuli.[29] This suggests that laboratory results are only the tip of the iceberg, since the most serious effects may occur after *many* repeated exposures. Marvin Wolfgang, a well-known sociologist, has also gone on record for reversing his previous opinion, and now declaring that the portrayal of violence encourages the increased use of aggression.[30]

It has been suggested that there are three reasons why a man might not commit rape. They are:

1. Social Controls: The fear of being caught and apprehended.
2. Social Norms: The definition of rape as unacceptable behavior.
3. Conscience: Some men abhor the idea of rape and view it as immoral and brutal behavior.[31]

Pornography undermines men's inhibitions against rape on all levels. In 1976, Don D. Smith did a content analysis of 28 "adults only" paperbacks (found in regular bookstores and newsstands) and published two studies. In the first, *The Social Content of Pornography*, he concluded that the world of pornography is a male world in which the male stereotype is "magnified tenfold." Men dominate every sexual activity, including portrayals of female homosexuality.[32] In the other work, *Sexual Aggression in American Pornography: The Stereotype of Rape*, three major themes are prominent:

1.   The victim really wants to be subjugated—forced to submit.
2.   Ashamed at her own gratification and recognition that she really liked what was done to her, the victim reports the act in less than 3 percent of the episodes.
3.   Less than 3 percent of the attackers meet with any negative consequences. Neither victim nor rapist is portrayed as having any regrets. The victim usually goes on to a richer, fuller sex life. Furthermore, in 97 percent of the rapes, the victim experiences orgasm and three-fourths of them experience multiple orgasm!

Smith notes that rape is depicted as being a part of normal female-male sexual relations and that his research supports much of Susan Brownmiller's findings.[33]

In *A Longitudinal Content Analysis of Sexual Violence in the Best-Selling Erotica Magazines*, 1973–1977, Neil Malamuth and Barry Spinner found that the amount of sexual violence portrayed had increased over the past 5 years. They indicate that the message in pornography is that women are masochistic and in need of male domination. They believe there is reason to become concerned over the fusion of sexuality and violence. This constant "coupling of sex and violence may involve conditioning processes whereby violent acts become associated with sexual pleasure, a highly powerful unconditioned stimulus and reinforcer."[34]

It appears to be true that geographical concentration of pornography is a factor involved with the incidence of sexual violence. For example, Los Angeles is undoubtedly one of the major producers and distributors of pornography. Police estimate sales in 1969 grossed $15 million, while in 1976 they had risen to $85 million. Is it a pure coincidence that rape has escalated most dramatically in Los Angeles? The following is a comment by Superintendent McAuley of the Los Angeles Police Department which describes new trends in rape that resemble the new wave of sadistic themes in pornography. " '. . . .Rapes are becoming more violent. The offenders are using more force, and we have noticed rapists are subjecting women to indecent acts far more than before.' "[35] J. H. Court, Ph.D., of Flinders University, concludes that the "high incidence of rape is occurring concurrently with the growth of pornography. The themes of pornography have a strong affinity to the philosophy of rape. There does not appear to be a case for arguing that a vicarious exposure to sexual gratification has reduced the likelihood of committing offenses, but rather to the contrary."[36]

On July 1st, 1969 pictorial pornography was legalized in Denmark. Extensive research was done to show there was a marked decrease in "sex offenses" committed there.[37] A closer look at the category of "sex offenses" revealed that rape was lumped with flashing, peeping, and other mild sex offenses. Rape was *not* one of the offenses that *decreased*, it in fact *increased*.[38] In addition, some sex offenses (voyeurism, for example) were decriminalized in Denmark in the interim. Also, after the laws were liberalized, attitudes toward sex offenses changed. This would very likely effect the reporting of rape, which pornography treats as a trivial matter.[39] In summary, research conducted to demonstrate a negative relationship between the incidence of sex offenses and the legalization of pornography has come under fire and has been largely disproven.[40]

Evidence is also emerging from the laboratory. In one study conducted by Dolf Zillmann and Jennings Bryant, 80 males and 80 females were subjected to massive, intermediate, nil, or no prior exposure to nonviolent pornography over a period of 6 weeks. The massive exposure group recommended significantly shorter terms of imprisonment for a crime of rape—making rape appear a trivial and inconsequential offense. This group indicated less support for the female liberation movement and the men had significantly higher sex-calloused attitudes toward women. The intermediate exposure groups scored somewhat lower than the massive exposure groups and higher than the other two groups. The authors stress that these effects were observed after viewing nonviolent depictions of sexual activity. They are thus concerned about the likely consequences of consistent exposure to pornography.[41]

Seymour Feshback and Neal Malamuth have demonstrated a link between sex and aggression through a common taboo against both sets of behaviors. They are concerned about the impact of pornography in which sexuality and violence are fused, as in sadomasochistic scenes. They conducted a series of studies in which they asked both men and women to read two versions of an erotic story; a few selected words were varied to make one passage aggressive, the other nonaggressive. Those who had read the more aggressive version reported feeling more sexually aroused than readers of the less aggressive version. In another study, they compared reactions to varied rape passages. Reading a rape story inhibited arousal responses in both men and women. The responses, however, depended upon whether the victim was perceived as being in pain or was perceived as enjoying the assault. For women, regardless of outcome, low arousal resulted. For men, however, initial inhibitions were reversed if the victim became sexually excited and high arousal resulted.[42] This finding is particularly frightening, because in pornography the victim is most often *enjoying* pain and assault.

Malamuth, Haber, and Feshbach conducted another study which addressed an issue discussed by Dr. Diana E. H. Russell. She proposed, on the basis of much research, that a large percentage of the adult male population has a propensity toward rape and assault. If they didn't, she argued, pornography could not have the impact it does on promoting violent behavior. In *The Politics of Rape* she suggested that we view sexual behavior as a continuum, with rape at one end and sex liberated from sex-role stereotyping at the other. Much of what passes as normal heterosexual intercourse would be seen as close to rape.

Malamuth explored the possibility that rape may be an extension of normal sexual patterns. Male subjects were given a passage to read, one version mildly sadomasochistic, the other nonviolent. They were then all given a common rape passage to read. By means of a second questionnaire, they discovered that males who read the sadomasochistic story previously tended to be more sexually excited in response to the account of rape than the others who had read the nonviolent version. The inhibitions which are normally a response to pain cues became inoperative after reading a sadomasochistic story in which women enjoyed being abused. For this group, the greater their judgment of pain, the greater the sexual excitement. Additionally, 51 percent of the men said they might rape as the man in the story did if they were assured of not being caught and punished.

Upon conclusion of their series of studies, Feshbach and Malamuth say that erotic violence has indeed become the central theme in pornography. "The message that pain and humiliation can be 'fun' encourage the relaxation of inhibitions against rape."[43] They add that "as psychologists, we would support community efforts to restrict violence in erotica to adults who are fully cognizant of the nature of the material and who choose knowingly to buy it." Further, they believe that "psychologists . . . ought not to support, implicitly or explicitly, the use and dissemination of violent erotic materials." Some have referred to this as an "inadequate policy recommendation . . . given their findings."[44]

In 1974, Yoram Jaffe, Neil Malamuth, Joan Feingold, and Seymour Feshbach demonstrated a link between sexuality and aggression. Sexually aroused males and females delivered more intensive shocks, regardless of gender of confederate or experimenter. In 1980, Malamuth and other colleagues went on to study the sexual responses of college students to rape depictions. They conducted a study which consisted of two experiments. In the first experiment it was found that the students were less sexually aroused by depictions of rape than mutually consenting sex. The second experiment found that portraying the victim as having orgasm disinhibited subjects' sexual responsiveness and resulted in levels of arousal comparable to the depiction of mutually consenting sex. It was also found that females were most aroused when the victim experienced an orgasm and no pain, but the males were most aroused when the victim experienced an orgasm *and* pain.[45]

Social psychologist Edward Donnerstein has also been engaged in some useful research on the effects of aggressive-erotic stimuli on male aggression towards females. One study consisted of 120 male subjects who were angered or treated neutrally by a male or female confederate. They were then shown a neutral, erotic, or aggressive-erotic film and given an opportunity to aggress against the confederate by delivery of electric shock. Results showed that the aggressive-erotic (A/E) film was effective in increasing aggression overall; however, it produced the greatest increase in aggression against females. Even the non-angered subjects showed an increase in aggression against the female after viewing an A/E film.

Donnerstein also reported that: (1) 50 percent of university females report some form of sexual aggression; (2) 39 percent of sex offenders questioned indicated that pornography had something to do with the crime committed; and (3) the incidence of rape and other sexual assault have increased. He calls for a systematic examination into the role of the media upon aggression against women, and concludes that: "There is ample evidence that the observation of violent forms of media can facilitate aggressive responses . . . , yet to assume that the depiction of sexual aggression could not have a similar effect, particularly against females, would be misleading."[46]

Donnerstein and Hallam demonstrated that exposure to erotic film can facilitate aggressive responses against females. In a similar study, male subjects were angered by a male or female confederate and exposed to an erotic film, an aggressive film, or no film condition. The subjects were given two opportunities to aggress. It was found that both the erotic and aggressive films increased aggression against females and males. The erotic film, however, facilitated aggression against females *both* times. In erotic films, as in violent pornography, women are shown in submissive positions. Females, being the targets of aggression, become associated with observed aggression. They conclude that films of both an erotic and an aggressive nature can be a mediator of aggression against women.[47] It seems Robin Morgan correctly summed up the situation back in the 1960s: "Pornography is the theory; rape is the practice."[48]

MEETING THE PROBLEM

The debate on the effects of pornography is not over; on the contrary, the debate is quickly becoming a raging battle. Feminists are divided in how to deal with pornography. One side views pornography as an assault on women's civil rights and demands some form of censorship; the other is the Feminists Anti-Censorship Taskforce (FACT) position which views censorship as a tool that will be abused; they therefore stand by the Amendment. Andrea Dworkin and Catharine A. Mackinnon drafted the "Model Anti-Pornography Law" upon which ordinances throughout the nation have been based. Their contention in writing this law was that pornography was a form of sex discrimination and is therefore unconstitutional and a civil rights violation which prohibits women from achieving equal status, and reduces women's opportunities in education, employment, and society. This law defines pornography as the combination of these situations:

- women are presented dehumanized as sexual objects, things, or commodities; or
- women are presented as sexual objects who enjoy pain or humiliation;
- women are presented as sexual objects who experience sexual pleasure in being raped; or
- women are presented as sexual objects tied up or cut up or mutilated or bruised or physically hurt; or
- women are presented in postures of sexual submission or sexual servility, including by inviting penetration; or
- women's body parts—including but not limited to vaginas, breasts, and buttocks—are exhibited, so that women are reduced to those parts; or
- women are presented being penetrated by objects or animals; or
- women are presented in scenarios of degradation, injury, or torture, shown as filthy or inferior, bleeding, bruised, or hurt, in a context that makes these conditions sexual.

Material must meet each part of the definition to be pornography. It must be sexually explicit and graphically depicted in pictures or in words, and it must contain at least one of the listed characteristics.

The legislative record from the hearings shows that it is the combination of these elements that contributes to injury and discrimination.

The definition excludes erotica that does not rely on the dynamic of submission and domination but is based on sexual equality. It also excludes material that contains scenes of sexual violence or force if the material does not itself subordinate women.[49]

Whether censorship is attained on a limited basis or not, the fact remains that there are many victims of pornography. From the models to the victims that aggression is displaced to, there is a great deal of pain and terror that must be addressed. Many issues need to be thought about. For example: What effect has pornography on the relationship between the sexes, upon body image and hence self-esteem, on human regard for others' integrity and physical and emotional well-being, on the coincidence of violence against women and children; and does pornography form children's basis for understanding their sexuality? Many of these issues have been the topic of research; others are philosophical in nature and cannot easily be answered with the scientific method. The question remains as to what concerned parties can do to combat effectively the infiltration of pornography into our lives. The fact that the industry is largely owned and operated by organized crime makes the task seem insurmountable. There are, however, several things that individuals can do:

1. Do not patronize magazines or movies that sexualize the victimization of other people either subtly or overtly.
2. Do not bring pornography into the home.
3. Boycott and write stores that sell pornography.
4. Educate others. Talk about the content and intent of pornographic displays.

The increase in domestic violence has correlated with the increase in the volume and violent content of the ever-expanding variety of pornography. Censorship in some form will probably be necessary to protect women and children, the victims of violent crimes, unless the consumers of pornography begin to realize what pornography is promoting and refuse to allow it the marketability it currently enjoys.

The world must be a safe, humanizing place for everyone. Publications or movies that promote the degradation and abuse of others have a large market. With vocalization, education, and even the legal system, the reduction or elimination of pornography is a very possible reality.

NOTES

1. Barkey, J. M. Minneapolis Debates Anti-Porn Law *Women Against Pornography, Newsreport*, 1984, Vol. VI, No. 1, p. 3.
2. *Women Against Pornography, Newsreport*, New York, 1986.

3. Schupper, A. Porn's Horatio Algers. *Mother Jones*, April 1980, Vol. V, No. 3, p. 32.
4. Ibid.
5. *Women Against Pornography, Newsreport*, op. cit.
6. Ibid.
7. Ibid.
8. Longino, H., Pornography, oppression and freedom: A closer look. In L. Lederer *Take back the night*, New York: William Morrow, 1980, p. 42.
9. Dworkin, A. *Pornography: Men possessing women*. New York: Pedigree Books, 1980, p. 200.
10. Eysenck, A., & Nias, D. K. B. *Sex, violence and the media*, New York: Harper & Row, 1978, p. 258.
11. Brownmiller, S. *Against our will: Men, women and rape*. New York: Simon & Schuster, 1975, p. 444.
12. Grager, N., & Shurr, C. *Sexual assault: Confronting rape in America*. New York: Grosset & Dunlap, 1976, p. 244.
13. Lederer, L. *Take back the night*. New York: William Morrow, 1980, p. 17.
14. Ibid., p. 18.
15. *Women against pornography, Newsreport*, Vol. VI, No. 1, Spring–Summer, 1984, p. 40.
16. Jones, A. A little knowledge, *Take back the night*, op cit. p. 179.
17. *Women against pornography, Newsreport*, 1986, op cit.
18. Berkowitz, L. Sex and violence: We can't have it both ways, *Psychology Today*, 1971. Vol. 5, pp. 14–23.
19. Cline, V. *Where do you draw the line?* Prova, Utah: Brigham Young University Press, 1973.
20. Fields, H. "Meese Panel Final Report Still Excepts Print-Only Material," Publishers Weekly, July 27, 1986, p. 16.
21. President's Commission on the Causes and Prevention of Violence, Washington, D.C., 1971, p. 23.
22. Ibid.
23. Bandura, A. *Aggression: A social learning analysis*, New York, Prentice-Hall, 1973.
24. Rushton, J. Effect of prosocial television and film material on the behavior of viewers, In L. Berkowitz, *Sex and Violence*.
25. Cline, V., op. cit., p. 208.

26. Feshbach, S. Mixing sex with violence—A dangerous form of alchemy, *New York Times*, Sunday, August 3, 1980.
27. Eysenck, H. J., and Nias, D. K. B., *Sex, Violence, and the Media.* New York: Harper and Row, 1978. p. 258.
28. Russell, D. H. Pornography and violence: What does the new research say, In *Take back the night*, p. 220.
29. Eysenck, H. Psychology is about people. In *Pornography: The longford report*, New York: Coronet Books, 1972.
30. Wolfgang, M. In *Take back the night*, op. cit. p. 237.
31. Ibid., p. 234.
32. Smith, D. D. The social content of pornography, *Journal of Communication*, Winter 1976, Vol. 26:1.
33. Smith, D. D. *Sexual aggression in American pornography: The stereotype of rape*, Paper presented at the Annual Meeting of the American Sociological Association, New York City, 1976.
34. Malamuth, N., & Spinner, B., *A longitudinal content analysis of sexual violence in the best-selling erotica magazines*, University of Manitoba: Presented at the Western Psychological Meetings. San Diego, California, April 1979.
35. DeLuca, G. Rape and pornography in Los Angeles. In Court, J. H., *Rape and pornography in Los Angeles.* Paper presented at annual conference for Australian Psychological Association, August 1977.
36. Court, J. H. Pornography and sex crimes: A re-evaluation in light of trends around the world. *International Journal of Criminology and Penology*, 1976, Vol. 5, pp. 129–157.
37. Bart P., & Jozsa, M. Dirty books, dirty films, and dirty data, In *Take back the night*, op. cit. p. 220.
38. Court, J. H. op. cit. pp. 129–157.
39. Zillman, D., & Bryant, J. Pornography, sexual callousness, and the trivialization of rape, *Journal of Communication*, Autumn 1982, Vol. 32, No. 4.
40. Court, J. H. op. cit., pp. 129–157.
41. Zillman, D., & Bryant, J., op. cit.
42. Malamuth, N., Haber, S., & Feshbach, S. Testing hypotheses regarding rape: Exposure to sexual violence, sex differences and the "normality" of rapists. *Journal of Research in Personality*, 1980, Vol. 14, pp. 121–137.
43. Ibid.

44. Bart P., & Jozsa, M. Dirty books, dirty films and dirty data. In *Take back the night*, op. cit. p. 216.

45. Malamuth, N., Heim, M., & Feshbach, S. Sexual responses of college students to rape depictions: Inhibitory and disinhibitory effects, *Journal of Personality and Social Psychology*, 1980, Vol. 38, No. 3, pp. 399–408.

46. Donnerstein, E. *Pornography Commission revisited: Aggression, erotica and violence against women*, University of Wisconsin, Unpublished and undated paper.

47. Donnerstein, E., & Hallam, J. Facilitating effects of erotica on aggression against women, *Journal of Personality and Social Psychology*, 1978, Vol. 36, No. 11, pp. 1270–1277.

48. Mogan, R. *Going too far: A personal chronicle of a feminist*, New York: Random House, 1977, p. 163.

49. Barkey, J. M. Minneapolis debates anti-porn law. *Woman Against Pornography, Newsreport*, 1984 Vol. VI, No. 1, p. 3.

Chapter 10

CONCLUSIONS

Nancy Hutchings

As we have seen, the American home is a violent setting. The greatest risk citizens of the United States run of being assaulted or physically injured is in their own homes, usually by members of their own families. Newspapers routinely report abused children and battered wives. When a crime, such as a murder, is traced to its origins it is often found that family violence is the primary cause. But, as we have also seen, many states are passing laws that mandate arrest of battering spouses and of parents that abuse children. The tradition that within the privacy of the home a husband or a parent exerts complete authority faces challenge—perhaps, as we have emphasized, not often enough—but with new awareness and new laws, change may be hoped for. Yet we are still dealing with only the tip of the iceberg as far as violence in the family is concerned.

It is widely accepted by social researchers, mental health professionals, and the legal institutions that violent offenses are still not widely reported. As Mullarkey points out in Chapter 3, family members who report crimes within their families are made to feel guilty and, often, that *they* are the cause of breakup of the family structure. The victim bears the blame.

The economic status of single women in the 1980s is so bleak that a wife who leaves her battering husband or takes children away from an abusing father may face insoluble problems. The recent book *Never Guilty, Never Free*[1] demonstrates the dilemma of the battered wife. She becomes so frightened and passive that leaving her husband never seems to be a rational choice for her. The traditional upbringing of many girls until the 1980s was that the role of wife meant subjugation to the husband's role, even to his battering.

The economic status of women reinforces this subjugation. The 1980s have been termed the decade of the feminization of poverty. The cuts in social programs under President Reagan have most harmed single elderly women and single female parents. Today's single mother with three children lives at *$3,000 below the poverty level.*[2] This is a mother who is receiving both federal and state public assistance. As detailed in Chapter 2, the theory of "less eligibility" in public assistance is to make public welfare a more appalling prospect than the lowest paying job! For women with young children, opportunities for employment are *only* in low-paying jobs and no adequate or quality day-care services exist for working mothers. The economic institutions that make policies regarding jobs, wages, and child care are controlled by *men,* who want to keep their decision-making positions. There is a drastic need for change in the welfare structure. The current number of single-parent families living below the poverty level will only cause an increase in crime and violence in the next generation. Our children, who are our most important resource, are being sacrificed by government policies in the 1980s that are ignoring their physical and emotional health.

Historically, violence has been supported by the church and by other legal institutions. Physical punishment of children was extolled by the Bible, and this legal prerogative assured parents, teachers, and guardians. The Society for the Prevention of Cruelty to Animals was established before the Society for the Prevention of Cruelty to Children.[3] Husbands also had legal sanction to use physical punishment to control their wives. English common law sanctioned the use of a switch to punish erring wives. The women's movement brought woman-battering to the attention of the

American public in the 1970s and initiated the formation of women's shelters beginning in 1965.[4] More recently, television and fiction have heightened society's awareness. However, to end much of the violence would take a fundamental change in the power structure of the family. As a first step, the economic structure would have to give more power to women.

Domestic violence cases that come into the legal system are on the rise; but the delays and legal processes tend to favor the battering husband, the rapist, or the child abuser. The civil rights of the accused perpetrator seem paramount in our legal system. The delays and the plea bargaining are emotionally trying to the mental health of the victims. When time has brought some healing to the victims, the case is finally brought to trial and there is a reopening of the traumatic experience. Today there are advocates for victims of crimes and certainly there is more understanding of their particular needs. Yet the court system still seems to favor the rights of the accused.

This book has included a chapter on rape though it is not usually considered—though it may be!—family violence. But the understanding of what happens to one's emotional well-being after a rape is important in comprehending the impact of all violence on the victim. Rape, of course, can occur in marriage. Oregon was the first state to pass a law in 1977 against such rape, and California and 18 other states have followed suit. In one survey, 14 percent of the women interviewed said that their husbands had raped them.[5] Again, this figure probably understates the incidence, since most wives would not accuse their husbands, and many of them would not participate in such a survey. The tradition that wives are the property of their husbands, plus the reinforcement by religious and social institutions that the role of women is to bear children, allows husbands the freedom to rape their wives.

The introductory chapter discussed how a patriarchal society reinforces the context in which a husband can force his wife and children into many behaviors. The balance of power in the family so favors the husband and father that it is not surprising when a spouse is accused of rape. Power often brings with it abuse of that power. In many states it remains legal for husbands to rape their wives, and it is important for mental health professionals to be aware that this form of violence exists. The chapters in this book have stressed the *questioning* and *listening* skills that are essential for all human service professionals, and rape in any relationship particularly calls for these skills.

Certainly, physical violence against wives and children has been well documented, and the sexual abuse of children has become a focus of the media. The general viewing and reading public is still perplexed as to the causes. Has there been a recent increase in incest and battering of wives? Is it just that there is a new awareness of problems that have always existed? Also, families now are revealing these problems to mental health workers, to the police and to the legal system. Possibly the attention of the media relieves victims of guilt and gives them a freedom to open up about family violence. It is also possible that the women's movement, and the approach of equality of the sexes has given a sense of greater power to women and children and encouraged them to tell the truth.

Pornography is another factor that may contribute to a rise in family violence. This is an opinion that is widely open to disserting theories. Is there proof that the increase in violence and pornography in the media has had an adverse effect on families? Certainly cable television, home videocassettes, and the popular movies of the 1980s are extremely violent. There are toys that glorify men who kill and there are lyrics to hit songs that stress violence and bizarre behavior. In 1986 a Presidential Commission investigating pornography as it relates to children and the law interestingly held no hearings on pornography and the issue of total family violence. The chairman of this Commission sought to close down pornographic bookstores as a protection for children, but overall media violence is being ignored.

The issues of free speech and anticensorship have always made pornography a conflicting issue in the United States, where we have stressed freedom for the media. Chapter 9 analyzed this question. It has to be recognized that family violence is increasing at the same time that media violence has dramatically increased; further research is therefore certainly necessary. The debate over censorship will continue, but the generation of children growing up in the 1980s will probably demonstrate the effects of the increase of violence in the media.

Social work and other mental health professions are caretaking and nurturing by their very nature; hence, the perspective of stressing the rights of women and children should come naturally. However, the patriarchal institutions of mental health practitioners often place the therapist in an authority position over the client. When a victim of family violence goes for professional counseling, she has to be in a situation of feeling equal, of being able to make her own decisions, and building her own self-esteem. Social work and the women's movement share important philosophical and value commitments[7] and the leading social workers early in the twentieth century were women. The inherent dignity of each human being and the client's right to self-determination are values basic to social workers and especially important for victims of violence. The social workers' understanding of systems theory and the importance of policy changes should encourage them to be leaders for better economic and legal institutions for women and children. Social workers must not be satisfied with helping a battered woman to adjust or cope with *her* situation; they need to help to change the overriding *situation* or to help the victim to gain the ego strengths to build a different life for herself.

In summing up the key themes in this book for all the helping professions, most specifically social work, it would seem that all the chapters register two prime points. First, there is a drastic need for a change in policies and present institutions if one is to prevent future family violence and to rescue its victims. Economic career equality for women so that they can leave violent marriages, and quality day-care programs for children when mothers attempt independence would be policies that would transform life for these now helpless families, and offer them a future. The legal system also should give more consideration to the rights of the victims; concern for protecting the civil rights of the accused should not sacrifice the civil rights of the defenseless not to be abused.

The second major theme of this book is that social workers and other professionals have to be willing to listen and to accept the *existence* of violence in a family. The value base that is brought into the profession by each individual may reject the incestuous parent, the violent husband, or the granny-basher, yet we cannot be helpful until we have opened our eyes and ears. Violence is rampant in the American family and all professionals have to unite to help to alleviate the suffering it inflicts. There has to be a commitment by all the helping professions to work for social change and to offer a dedication of their own personal skills to working with the victims of violence.

NOTES

1. Foat, G., with Foreman, L. *Never guilty, never free.* New York: Random House, 1985.
2. *Social Security Bulletin,* August 1981, Vol. 27, Issue 16.
3. Straus, M. A., Gelles, R. J., & Steinmetz, S. K. *Behind closed doors: Violence in the American family.* Garden City, Anchor Press, 1980. p. 8.
4. Martin, D. *Battered wives.* New York: Pocket Books, p. 198.
5. Russell, D. E. H. *Rape in marriage.* New York: Macmillan, 1982, p. 2.
6. VanGelder, L., Pornography goes to Washington. *Ms.* magazine, New York: Ms. Foundation, June 1986, p. 52.
7. Collins, B. G., Defining feminist social work, *Social Work,* National Association of Social Workers, Silver Springs, MD, May–June 1986, Vol. 31, No. 3, p. 215.

APPENDIX

197 N. J. Super.	State v. Sheppard.
	Cite as, 197 N. J. Super. 411

STATE OF NEW JERSEY, PLAINTIFF, v. GEORGE R. SHEPPARD, DEFENDANT.

Superior Court of New Jersey
Law Division (Criminal)
Burlington County

Decided August 29, 1984.

SYNOPSIS

In prosecution of defendant for sexual assault, engaging in sexual conduct which would impair or debauch morals of a child, and child abuse, State moved for permission to present testimony of ten-year-old victim through use of video equipment, and defendant objected, claiming his right of confrontation would be violated by the procedure. The Superior Court, Law Division,

State v. Sheppard.   *197 N. J. Super.*
Cite as, 197 N. J. Super. 411

Burlington County, Haines, A.J.S.C., held that: (1) use of videotape testimony of child victim would be permitted, and (2) defendant waived his right of confrontation by making threats to victim.

Motion to present testimony of child victim of sexual assault through use of video equipment granted.

---

1. Criminal Law ⟜ 662.1
   Confrontation clause declares a fundamental right to which the states are subject by reason of the Fourteenth Amendment. U.S.C.A. Const. Amends. 6, 14.

2. Criminal Law ⟜ 662.1
   Constitutional right of confrontation is not absolute. U.S.C.A. Const. Amend. 6.

3. Criminal Law ⟜ 438(8)
   Videotape records fall within definition of "writing" in the rules of evidence, for purposes of determining whether videotapes are admissible in evidence. Rules of Evid., N.J.S.A. 2A:84A, Rule 1(13).

4. Criminal Law ⟜ 662.3, 667(1)
   In determining whether to allow testimony of ten-year-old sexual assault victim to be presented through use of video equipment, court must weigh great harm to victims of child abuse, inability to prosecute child abusers because evidence against them cannot be presented, and damage to children by traumatic role in testifying in court against defendant's right of confrontation. U.S.C.A. Const. Amend. 6.

5. Criminal Law ⟜ 662.3, 667(1)
   Child victim would be allowed to testify through use of video equipment in prosecution for sexual assault, engaging in sexual conduct which would impair or debauch the morals of a child and child abuse, despite resulting lack of eye contact between witness and defendant and defendant's claim of a confrontation clause

violation, where defendant, judge, jury and spectators would see and hear the child clearly, where adequate opportunity for cross-examination would be provided, and in view of court's finding of harm to child if she was required to testify in court; disagreeing with *U.S. v. Benfield*, 593 F.2d 815. U.S.C.A. Const. Amend. 6; N.J.S.A. Const. Art. 1, par. 10.

6. Criminal Law ⊨ 662.7
Confrontation clause's central purpose is provision of the opportunity for cross-examination. U.S.C.A. Const. Amend. 6; N.J.S.A. Const. Art. 1, par. 10.

7. Witnesses ⊨ 268(1)
Like the right of confrontation, the right of cross-examination is not without limitations. U.S.C.A. Const. Amend. 6; N.J.S.A. Const. Art. 1, par. 10.

8. Criminal Law ⊨ 662.80
A defendant may waive his Sixth Amendment right of confrontation. U.S.C.A. Const. Amend. 6; N.J.S.A. Const. Art. 1, par. 10.

9. Criminal Law ⊨ 777
Evidence rule, providing that if a judge admits a statement, he shall not inform the jury that he has made a finding that the statement is admissible, and he shall instruct the jury that they are to disregard the statement if they find it is not credible, but if the judge subsequently determines that the statement is not admissible, he shall take appropriate action, is applicable only when statement concerned is a statement which is intended to be introduced at trial. Rules of Evid., N.J.S.A. 2A:84A, Rule 8(1, 3).

10. Criminal Law ⊨ 632(5)
Rule of evidence, providing that if a judge admits a statement he shall not inform jury that he has made a finding that the statement is admissible, and shall instruct jury that they are to disregard statement if they find it not credible, but if judge subsequently determines from all evidence that statement is not

State v. Sheppard.   *197 N. J. Super.*
Cite as, 197 N. J. Super. 411

admissible he shall take appropriate action, did not apply to
admissibility of psychiatrist's testimony at pretrial hearing
regarding threats sexual assault defendant allegedly made to child
victim, for purposes of determining whether victim's videotape
testimony would be admissible without consideration of defendant's
right to confrontation. U.S.C.A. Const. Amend. 6; N.J.S.A. Const.
Art. 1, par. 10; Rules of Evid., N.J.S.A. 2A:84A, Rule 8(1, 3).

11. Criminal Law ∞ 667(1)
Psychiatrist's testimony regarding defendant's threat to kill
child victim was admissible at pretrial hearing in prosecution for
sexual assault, engaging in sexual conduct which would impair
or debauch morals of a child, and child abuse for purposes of
determining whether defendant waived his right to confrontation
by reason of such threats, and thus, whether victim would be able
to testify through use of video equipment. U.S.C.A. Const. Amend.
6; N.J.S.A. Const. Art. 1, par. 10.

12. Criminal Law ∞ 662.80
Standard for determining whether a defendant waived his right
to confrontation by threatening a victim is preponderance of the
evidence. U.S.C.A. Const. Amend. 6; N.J.S.A. Const. Art. 1, par.
10.

13. Criminal Law ∞ 662.80
In prosecution for sexual assault, engaging in sexual conduct
which would impair or debauch morals of a child, and child abuse,
the state supported with sufficient evidence its claim that defendant
waived his right to confrontation by threatening to kill the child
victim, despite fact that evidence of defendant's threat to kill victim
was hearsay consisting of victim's statement to a psychiatrist and
repeated by him at a pretrial hearing, where child's statement to
the psychiatrist was made in a setting of confidence, and was not
made because child knew that her statement could effect a waiver
of the confrontation clause; under the circumstances, defendant
waived his right to confrontation with the child victim, and victim's
testifying through use of videotape equipment was permissible.
U.S.C.A. Const. Amend. 6; N.J.S.A. Const. Art. 1, par. 10.

---

197 N. J. Super.   State v. Sheppard.
                Cite as, 197 N. J. Super. 411

Lily Oeffler for plaintiff (*Stephen G. Raymond*, Burlington County Prosecuting Attorney).

Robert Sloan for defendant (*James Logan, Jr.*, attorney).

HAINES, A.J.S.C.

Defendant, George R. Sheppard, has been indicted for sexual assault, engaging in sexual conduct which would impair or debauch the morals of a child and child abuse. The State now moves for permission to present the testimony of the ten-year-old victim, defendant's stepdaughter, through the use of video equipment. Defendant objects, claiming his right of confrontation, guaranteed by the Sixth Amendment of the *United States Constitution* and Art. 1, par. 10 of the *New Jersey Constitution* (1947), will be violated by the procedure. The question has not been addressed in the published opinion of any court in this State.[1]

The State proposes to place the child, the prosecuting attorney, defense counsel, and a cameraman in a room near the courtroom at the time of trial. The room will be equipped with video and audio systems. The judge, jury, and defendant will be in the courtroom. The child will testify as though sitting in the courtroom, responding to questions from the prosecutor and the defense attorney. Defendant, the judge, the jury, and the public will see and hear her testimony through monitors placed appropriately in the courtroom. Private communication between defendant and his attorney will be available through an audio connection.

A hearing was held, in response to the State's application, at which witnesses for the State testified and were cross-examined. Defendant, who was present, represented by counsel and provided with notice and an opportunity to be heard, did not introduce any evidence.

---

[1]It has been addressed by Judge Edwin H. Stern in a New Jersey murder case. He permitted the use of video equipment in that case, stating his reasons from the bench. The transcript of his opinion has been supplied to counsel and the court.

State v. Sheppard.   *197 N. J. Super.*
Cite as, 197 N. J. Super. 411

Robert L. Sadoff, a forensic psychiatrist with substantial credentials relating to trial proceedings as well as medical matters, was the first witness. He interviewed the child victim for the purpose of testifying at the hearing. She revealed frequent incidents of sexual abuse by her stepfather beginning when she was only three or four years old. She told him she would be able to testify in open court facing the defendant. Her willingness, however, was based upon a misconception. She was afraid of her stepfather, who had threatened to kill her if she revealed his activities, and therefore wanted to send him to jail for her protection. She believed that he could not be sentenced to jail if she testified through the use of videotape equipment. When advised otherwise, she expressed a preference for a video arrangement.

Doctor Sadoff said the victim had the capacity to testify truthfully. It was his opinion, however, that avoidance of an in-court appearance through the use of video equipment would improve the accuracy of her testimony. He provided reasons: An adult witness, testifying in court, surrounded by the usual court atmosphere, aware of a black-robed judge, a jury, attorneys, members of the public, uniformed attendants, a flag, and religious overtones, is more likely to testify truthfully. The opposite is true of a child, particularly when the setting involves a relative accused by her of sexual abuse. She becomes fearful, guilty, anxious, and traumatized. In most cases, she will have been exposed to both pleasant and abusive associations with the accused. As a consequence, she has ambivalent feelings. Anger against the relative is opposed by feelings of care, not only for him but also for other family members who may be harmed by a conviction. There is guilt as well as satisfaction in the prospect of sending the abuser to prison. These mixed feelings, accompanied by the fear, guilt, and anxiety, mitigate the truth, producing inaccurate testimony. The video arrangement, because it avoids courtroom stress, relieves these feelings, thereby improving the accuracy of the testimony.

In his opinion, the child was well-oriented, with a sound memory and no evidence of psychotic-thought disorder, hallucinations or delusions. She currently receives group and individual

counseling. Probable long-range emotional consequences resulting
from her in-court testimony would be the continued presence of
fear, guilt, and anxiety. The testimonial experience is itself traumatic
and likely to be long remembered. Possible long-term effects of
her testimony in court would be nightmares, depression, eating,
sleeping, and school problems, behavioral difficulties, including
"acting out," and sexual promiscuity. The psychiatric goal in these
cases is to provide appropriate treatment of the offender and strong
support for the child to the end that the family can be reunited.
The prospect of reaching this goal will be much inhibited by face-
to-face testimony.

Two attorneys with substantial experience in the prosecution
of child abuse cases testified to the difficulties attending the
presentation of children's testimony. In most cases, prosecutions
are abandoned or result in generous plea agreements, either because
the child's emotional condition prevents her from testifying or
makes the testimony obviously inaccurate or inadequate. One
attorney, who had handled 30 to 40 of these cases for the State,
was able to complete a trial in only one. In most, while the child
victim was able to provide her with information sufficient to
support a prosecution and was sometimes able to appear with
difficulty before a grand jury, she could not testify in court face-
to-face with the accused and other relatives. The victim either refused
to testify or "froze" when she got to court. Children who did testify,
e.g., before a grand jury, frequently "forgot" details, changed stories,
or presented inconsistent facts. Ultimately, many broke down, cried,
ignored questions and eventually refused to answer. Most of the
victims involved in these cases were being treated by counsellors
who frequently advanced the opinion that their child patients could
not survive the trauma attending a courtroom appearance.

The second attorney, a member of a "charge" committee in
the prosecutor's office, had reviewed 75 to 80 cases of child abuse.
His committee was responsible for double-checking cases which
the prosecutor believed would have to be dismissed for various
reasons. Nearly 90% of the child abuse cases were dismissed as a
result of problems attending the testimony of children, who could

---

State v. Sheppard.   *197 N. J. Super.*
Cite as, 197 N. J. Super. 411

---

not deal with the prospect of facing fathers, stepfathers, relatives, and strangers in a courtroom setting. He described three child abuse cases which illustrated the problems.

(1) A child was the victim of a stranger's sexual molestation at age 12. The facts did not become known to the prosecutor (often the case) until she was 17. The case was dismissed on the basis of psychiatric advice that the child could not testify without having a total emotional breakdown. The child's approach to emotional survival, typically, had been to forget, forget, forget. Reinforcing her memory of this traumatic event would have been devastating.

(2) A seven-year-old boy was abused by a friend. He was precocious and articulate when speaking to the prosecuting attorney. When presented to the grand jury, the presence of many people made him hesitant, forgetful, and inconsistent. Shortly afterward, for unknown reasons, he and his family moved to Italy and the matter was resolved by a plea agreement.

(3) A father was charged with sexually abusing his daughter. The child found it very difficult to articulate the facts, and refused to discuss them with anyone except the prosecuting attorney. The complaint was therefore dismissed; the necessary facts could not be presented to a grand jury.

The final witness was a video expert. He testified that the video equipment to be used at the trial of this matter would provide instant transmission of images and voices from a remote room to the courtroom, providing more than acceptable clarity. Both video and audio would be taped to preserve the record of the child's testimony. Images could be presented in black and white or color. In the present case, color will be used. Special lighting is not necessary. Although bright lights improve color presentation, they will not be required in this case. Monitors (picture screens with sound capacities) will be connected to the camera and placed in the courtroom. A zoom lens will be available for close-ups of the witness. The witness and both attorneys can be photographed simultaneously without difficulty.

An in-court demonstration was provided by the expert using the video equipment to be employed at trial in a conference room adjoining the courtroom. Two attorneys acted as witness and prosecutor. A monitor with a 25" screen faced the judge. The use of the zoom lens was illustrated. A well-defined picture appeared on the monitor; when the zoom lens was used, facial details were provided with great clarity. The testimony was distinct and easily understood. The color was satisfactory although no special lighting was used. The video expert testified that audio communication between the defendant and his attorney would be provided through wireless devices or a hard wire connection. Two-way communication from the judge to the conference room could also be provided.

It is the court's conclusion that the planned video arrangement for presenting the testimony of the child victim satisfies constitutional requirements. It will be allowed. That conclusion is supported by the following extended analysis.

A. The Dimensions of the Problem; Trial Effects; Social Responsibility.

According to an extensive article appearing in *Newsweek* (May 14, 1984), "somewhere between 100,000 and 500,000 American children will be [sexually] molested this year." The same article refers to a study "showing that 19% of all American women and 9% of all men were sexually victimized as children." According to the State's witnesses in this matter, the Burlington County Prosecutor's Office interviews seven to eight children a month in connection with sexual-abuse cases. The *Newsweek* article discusses the difficulties involved when these cases reach court, pointing to many of the problems mentioned by the State's witnesses. Children and relatives are ashamed and afraid. There is anxiety about the future of the child and the family. In many cases the abuser contributes all or most of their financial support. Counselors who believe that rehabilitation and the consequent preservation of family unity and security are possible, advise against prosecution.

State v. Sheppard.   *197 N. J. Super.*
Cite as, 197 N. J. Super. 411

For obvious reasons, only one witness with personal knowledge is available to prove the State's case in almost every child abuse prosecution: the child victim. These victims, as shown by the State's proofs, have been traumatized by their subjection to the abuse. They become so further traumatized by the prospect of testifying in front of their abusers that they cannot speak about the central happenings or can do so only with great difficulty and doubtful accuracy. The in-court experience may cause further lasting emotional harm. Writers in the field bear this out. Libai, "The Protection of the Child Victim of a Sexual Offense in the Criminal Justice System," 15 *Wayne L. Rev.* 977 (1969), has this to say:

> Psychiatrists have identified components of the legal proceedings that are capable of putting a child victim under prolonged mental stress and endangering his emotional equilibrium: repeated interrogations and cross-examination, facing the accused again, the official atmosphere in court, the acquittal of the accused for want of corroborating evidence to the child's trustworthy testimony, and the conviction of a molester who is the child's parent or relative. [at 984]

> . . . .

> The fact is that psychiatrists all over the world repeatedly warn that 'legal proceedings are not geared to protect the victim's emotions and may be exceptionally traumatic.' The studies do not as yet demonstrate a clear causal link between the legal proceedings and the child victim's mental disturbances, but no psychiatric study has attempted to prove, or is likely to attempt to prove in the future, such a causal link. Psychiatrists agree that they cannot isolate the effects of the 'crime trauma' from the '*prior personality damage*' or either of the foregoing from the '*environment reaction trauma*' or the '*legal process trauma*.' But psychiatrists do agree that when some victims encounter the law enforcement system, for one reason or another, the child requires special care and treatment. [at 1015]

---

197 N. J. Super.   State v. Sheppard.
                      Cite as, 197 N. J. Super. 411

Libai points to a study comparing a "court sample" of child victims involved in criminal proceedings with a random sample of such victims, which "found that 73% of the court sample had behavior problems and over-disturbances compared with only 57% of the random sample." At 982.

Another article entitled, "Proving Parent-Child Incest," 15 *U. of Mich. Journal of Law Reform* 131 (Fall 1981), by Ordway, addresses the need to find a better way to present children's testimony in sexual abuse cases because of the human and social costs involved:

> Our system of justice manifests a concern with human costs at many levels. The eighth amendment prohibits cruel and unusual punishment, and prisons, despite their problems, attempt to provide for more than mere physical survival. Bankruptcy procedures protect enough of the assets to cover necessaries. Tort law struggles to develop a fair system for compensating victims' loss of companionship and mental distress. Most pertinent here are the informal procedures and the 'best interest' standards of the juvenile/family courts.
>
> Furthermore, it is as sensible to establish an exception to protect the incest victim from trauma as it is to protect the taxpayer from expenditure and the accused from delay. The only difference between the first and the latter two harms is the value at risk. In light of the fact that money and time have recognizable value only in relation to human needs and values, the cost in harm to a person must be valued at least as highly as money and time. [at 148, n. 78]

New Jersey is sensitive to the needs of juveniles and to their problems. Its system of juvenile courts, culminating in the recent creation of the Family Division of the Superior Court, has always been devoted to the "best interest" of the juvenile. Judicial responsibility in juvenile matters is described in *Sorentino v. Family & Children's Soc. of Elizabeth*, 72 *N.J.* 127 (1976), a custody case. The Supreme Court said:

State v. Sheppard.   *197 N. J. Super.*
Cite as, 197 N. J. Super. 411

The court cannot evade its responsibility, as *parens patriae*
of all minor children, to preserve them from harm. The
possibility of serious psychological harm to the child in this
case transcends all other issues. [at 132; citations omitted]

Unfortunately, this all-encompassing concern for the welfare of
children has not been directed toward their protection in our courts
when they are obliged to testify as victims of abuse.

Testimonial problems are being addressed in other states in
various ways. In California, for example, preliminary hearings may
be videotaped and the taped testimony presented at a later trial.
Cal. Penal Code § 1346 (West 1984). The arrangement, however,
does not resolve the problems of fear, anxiety, and trauma affecting
the child witness. She is still subjected to a face-to-face confrontation
at the preliminary hearing.

Some states permit hearsay testimony, *e.g.*, by a counsellor,
to avoid the presentation of a child witness. Videotaping
arrangements are authorized in some jurisdictions. Libai, *op. cit.*,
supra, recommends the use of a two-way glass enclosure in the
courtroom which would permit a child witness to be observed by
everyone in the courtroom while she remained unconscious of their
presence. Statutory provisions in addition to California which
illustrates the varied approaches are as follows:

(1) *Arizona*
    Permits videotaped testimony of a minor witness in the
presence of the court, the defendant, defendant's counsel, the
prosecuting attorney or plaintiff and plaintiff's counsel for
presentation to the jury at a later time as evidence. *Ariz. Rev.
Stat. Ann.* § 12–2312 (1982)

(2) *Florida*
    Upon application to the court on notice to the defendant
and proof of a substantial likelihood that a child abuse victim

will suffer severe emotional or mental strain if required to testify in open court, her out-of-court testimony may be videotaped for use as evidence. A trial judge must preside at the videotape session and shall rule on all questions as if at trial. (No mention is made of confrontation.) *Fla. Stat. Ann.* § 918.17 (West 1984)

(3) *Montana*

Videotaped testimony of a child victim is permissible as evidence even though the victim is not in the courtroom when the videotape is admitted into evidence. The judge, prosecuting attorney, victim, defendant, defendant's attorney, and such other persons as the court deems necessary shall be allowed to attend the videotaped proceedings. *Mont. Code Ann.* § 46-15-401 (1983)

(4) *New Hampshire*

In cases where the victim is under 16 years of age, the victim's testimony shall be heard in-camera unless good cause is shown by the defendant. The record of the victim's testimony is not to be sealed and all other testimony and evidence produced during the proceeding shall be public. *N.H. Rev. Stat. Ann.* § 632-A:8 (1983).

(5) *New Mexico*

Upon a showing that a child victim may be unable to testify without suffering unreasonable and unnecessary emotional or mental harm, out-of-court videotaping of her testimony is permitted. (No mention of confrontation.) *N.M. Stat. Ann.* § 30-9-17 (1982).

(6) *Colorado*

An out-of-court statement made by a child describing any act of sexual contact performed with that child which is otherwise inadmissible as evidence, is admissible in criminal proceedings in which the child is the victim of an unlawful sexual offense. The court must find that the statement is reliable and the child must either testify at the proceeding or be unavailable. *Colo. Rev. Stat.* § 13-25-129 (1983).

(7) *Washington*
     Same as Colorado's statute except that, when the child
is unavailable, there must be other corroborative evidence of
the act.

(8) *Texas*
     The "visual and aural" recording of the pretrial statement
of a child is admissiblè at trial if no attorney for either party
is present when the statement was made and the child is
available to testify. Other conditions are listed. If the statement
is admitted into evidence, either party may call the child to
testify and the opposing party may cross-examine. Statute
also permits testimony of a child by closed-circuit television
from a room outside the courtroom. "The court shall permit
the defendant to observe and hear the testimony of the child
in person but shall ensure that the child cannot hear or see
the defendant." In addition, statute permits a like arrangement
for recording the child's testimony before trial and its later
showing in court. *Tex. Crim. Proc. Code Ann.* § 38.071
(Vernon 1983).

     Texas appears to be the only state with a complete statutory
solution to the confrontation problem. Colorado and Washington
offer partial solutions since the admission of a "statement" is
obviously much less satisfactory than the presentation of all of
a child's testimony by videotape.

B. The Right of Confrontation: Physical Presence.
     [1]   The defendant claims that the proposed video presentation
of testimony violates his constitutional right of confrontation. It
is his reading of our constitutions that they entitle him to confront
every witness against him in person in court. The Sixth Amendment
to the *Constitution of the United States* provides in part: "in all
criminal prosecutions, the accused shall enjoy the right . . . to be
confronted with the witnesses against him. . . ." Art. 1, par. 10,
of the *New Jersey Constitution* (1947) provides: "in all criminal
prosecutions the accused shall have the right . . . to be confronted

with the witnesses against him. . . ." The confrontation clause is
held to be a fundamental right to which the states are subject
by reason of the Fourteenth Amendment. *Pointer v. Texas*, 380
U.S. 400, 403–405, 85 *S.Ct.* 1065, 1067–1069, 13 *L.Ed.*2d 923 (1965);
State v. Williams, 182 *N.J. Super.* 427, 434 (App. Div. 1982).
U.S. v Benfield, 593 *F.* 2d 815 (8 Cir. 1979), provides some
support for the defendant's position. In that case, after a videotaped
deposition of the victim was admitted into evidence, the defendant
was convicted of misprison of felony for failing to report an
abduction by others. The victim testified by deposition because
she feared psychological harm, if forced to confront the defendant
in court. During the deposition the defendant could observe the
victim through a one-way glass. He could reach his attorney, who
was present while the witness was deposed, through an audio device.
He appealed his conviction, arguing that his confrontation was
only partial and did not satisfy the Sixth Amendment. The appellate
court agreed, stating:

> Normally the right of confrontation includes a face-to-
> face meeting at trial at which time cross-examination takes
> place. . . . While some recent cases use other language, none
> denies that confrontation required a face-to-face meeting in
> 1791 and none lessens the force of the sixth amendment. Of
> course, confrontation requires cross-examination in addition
> to a face-to-face meeting. The right of cross-examination
> reinforces the importance of physical confrontation. Most
> believe that in some undefined but real way recollection,
> veracity and communication are influenced by face-to-face
> challenge. This feature is a part of the sixth amendment right
> additional to the right of cold, logical cross-examination by
> one's counsel. While a deposition necessarily eliminates a face-
> to-face meeting between witness and jury, we find no
> justification for further abridgment of the defendant's rights.
> A videotaped deposition supplies an environment substan-
> tially comparable to a trial, but where the defendant was not

State v. Sheppard.   *197 N. J. Super.*
Cite as, 197 N. J. Super. 411

permitted to be an active participant in the video deposition,
this procedural substitute is constitutionally infirm. [at 821]

Benfield, however, is distinguishable. It concerned a
deposition. The jury was not present to see and hear the actual
testimony. The victim was an adult, not a child, as here. The charge
did not involve sexual abuse. Furthermore, *Benfield* recognized the
possibility of exceptions to the right of confrontation, saying: "what
curtailment or diminishment might be constitutionally permissible
depends on the factual context of each case, including the
defendant's conduct . . . Any exception should be narrow in scope
and based on necessity or waiver." *Ibid.* Indeed, the court
acknowledged:

> It is possible that face-to-face confrontation through two-
> way closed circuit television might be adequate. By a four
> to three vote, the Missouri Supreme Court has approved the
> use of such testimony by an expert witness in a case involving
> violation of a municipal ordinance, despite a defense based
> on the sixth amendment. *Kansas City v. McCoy*, 525 S. W.
> 2d 336 (Mo. 1975). Among the more disturbing aspects of
> the decision is that there was no showing of extraordinary
> circumstances necessitating reliance on the procedure. [*Id.* at
> 822]

Defendant may obtain some comfort from *Herbert v. Superior
Court of the State of California*, 172 Cal. Rptr. 850, 117 Cal. App.
3d 661 (Dist. Ct. App. 1981). Defendant in that case was charged
with sexual offenses involving a five-year-old girl. At a preliminary
examination, she was reluctant or unable to testify and was therefore
so positioned in the courtroom that she and the defendant could
not see each other. The defendant could hear her testimony. She
could be seen by the judge and the attorneys. The court held that
the arrangement violated the defendant's right of confrontation,
citing *Benfield*. It said:

197 N. J. Super.	State v. Sheppard.
	Cite as, 197 N. J. Super. 411

The historical concept of the right of confrontation has included the right to see one's accused face-to-face, thereby giving the fact finder the opportunity of weighing the demeanor of the accused when forced to make his or her accusation before the one person who knows if the witness is truthful. [172 *Cal. Rptr.* at 855, 117 *Cal. App.* 3d at 671]

Herbert is closer to the point than *Benfield*. Nevertheless, it is also distinguishable. Here, the defendant will be able to see the witness; there he could not. The *Herbert* court recognized the fact that "[t]he confrontation right is not absolute," 172 *Cal. Rptr.* at 853, 117 *Cal. App.* 3d at 667, but found no room for an exception on the facts of that case. Its final conclusion was motivated in part by the fact that there was no record showing that the child's conduct required the arrangement, no record of any intimidating action by defendant, no oath taken by the victim and no request from defendant or the prosecutor to make a special arrangement. 172 *Cal. Rptr.* at 855, 117 *Cal. App.* 3d at 670. Here we have a record of the child's concerns, supported by the opinion of a psychiatrist who believed that emotional damage could be caused by in-court testimony. There has been a request by the prosecutor for the video arrangement. The witness will be sworn before she testifies. *Herbert* considered neither a video technique nor the special problems of child witnesses.

Additionally, doubt may be cast upon the *Herbert* conclusion by *Parisi v. Superior Court of the State of California for the County of Los Angeles*, 192 *Cal. Rptr.* 486, 144 Cal. App. 3d 211 (Dist. Ct. App. 1983). Defendant in that case was charged with sexual abuse of his eight-year-old daughter. The child appeared as a witness at the preliminary examination but became embarrassed and could not answer questions out loud. She was therefore permitted to whisper her answers to the magistrate conducting the hearing who repeated them on the record. Defendant argued that his rights of confrontation and cross-examination were impermissibly infringed by this procedure. The court, disagreeing, said:

State v. Sheppard.   *197 N. J. Super.*
Cite as, 197 N. J. Super. 411

It is the responsibility of every court to conduct its
proceedings in such a manner that the truth will be established
and it is its duty to render assistance whenever such aid is
needed.

In the case at bar, because of her fear and discomfort,
a young victim of sexual crimes committed by her father was
too embarrassed to articulate aloud answers to two most
intimate questions. Under such circumstances, it was not
improper for the magistrate to intervene in order to help elicit
her testimony. In essence, the court did but act as a "loud
speaker" for a child temporarily rendered mute. [at 192 *Cal.
Rptr.* 490; citations omitted]

The Court distinguished *Herbert* noting that the *Parisi* defendant
was able to see the witness.

[2] As *Benfield, Herbert,* and *Parisi* all acknowledged, the
right of confrontation is not absolute. *Benfield* and *Herbert* do
not control the issue in the present case. Other cases and other
reasons compel the conclusion here that the proposed video
presentation will not offend any constitutional demands.

As early as 1895, the United States Supreme Court held that
the right of confrontation "must occasionally give way to
considerations of public policy and the necessities of the case."
Mattox v. U.S., 156 *U.S.* 237, 243, 15 *S. Ct.* 337, 340, 39 *L.Ed.*
409 (1895). In *Mattox,* witnesses died and were consequently
unavailable[2] at the time of trial. Their prior testimony was admitted
into evidence. The Supreme Court held this to be permissible,
saying:

A technical adherence to the letter of a constitutional
provision may occasionally be carried further than is necessary
to the just protection of the accused, and further than the

---

[2]*Evid. R.* 63(3) permits prior testimony of an unavailable witness.
It does not fit the circumstances of this case.

| 197 N. J. Super. | State v. Sheppard. |
| | Cite as, 197 N. J. Super. 411 |

safety of the public will warrant. [156 *U.S.* at 243, 15 *S. Ct.* at 340]

In 1980, in *Ohio v. Roberts*, 448 *U.S.* 56, 100 *S. Ct.* 2531, 65 *L. Ed.* 2d 597 (1980), the Court said:

> [T]he Confrontation Clause reflects a preference for face-to-face confrontation at trial and that "a primary interest secured by [the provision] is the right to cross-examination," *Douglas v. Alabama*, 380 *U.S.* 415, 418 [85 *S. Ct.* 1074, 1076, 13 *L. Ed.* 2d 934] (1965)
>
> The Court, however, has recognized that competing interests, if closely examined, may warrant dispensing with confrontation at trial. [448 *U.S.* at 63–64, 100 *S. Ct.* at 2537–2538]

In *California v. Green*, 399 *U.S.* 149, 90 *S. Ct.* 1930, 26 *L. Ed.* 2d 489 (1970), Harlan, J. concurring, said: The belief that the rights of confrontation and cross-examination are co-extensive is "an understandable misconception." *Id.* at 172–173, 90 *S. Ct.* at 1942–1943.

Earlier, in *Douglas v. Alabama*, 380 *U.S.* 415,85 *S. Ct.* 1074, 13 *L. Ed.* 2d 934 (1965), the Court held:

> Our cases construing the clause hold that a primary interest secured by it is the right of cross-examination; an adequate opportunity for cross-examination may satisfy the clause even in the absence of physical confrontation. [380 *U.S.* at 418, 85 *S. Ct.* at 1076]

In *United States v. Tortora*, 464 *F.* 2d 1202 (2 Cir. 1972), *cert. den.* 409 *U.S.* 1063, 93 *S. Ct.* 554, 34 *L. Ed.* 2d 516 (1972), the voluntary failure of a defendant to appear in court was held to waive his right of confrontation. In *United States v. Toliver*, 541 *F.* 2d 958 (2 Cir. 1976), an asthmatic defendant was absent during several days of trial while prosecution witnesses testified. The court nevertheless held that such testimony, while violating the confrontation clause, was not sufficiently probative of the defendant's guilt to constitute reversible error. In *Dutton v. Evans*, 400 *U.S.* 74, 91 *S. Ct.* 210, 27 *L. Ed.* 2d 213 (1970), the Court permitted introduction of an out-of-court statement, holding that there was no violation of the confrontation clause because the testimony had other "indicia of reliability," was of "peripheral significance" and was not "crucial" to the prosecution or "devastating" to the defendant. *Id.* at 87, 91 *S. Ct.* at 219.

5 *Wigmore, Evidence* (Chadbourne Rev. 1974) § 1365, discusses the distinction between confrontation and cross-examination:

> Now confrontation is, in its main aspect, *merely another term for the test of cross-examination.* It is the preliminary step to securing the opportunity of cross-examination; and, so far as it is essential, this is only because cross-examination is essential. The right of confrontation is the right to the opportunity of cross-examination. Confrontation also involves a subordinate and incidental advantage, namely, the observation by the tribunal of the witness' demeanor on the stand, as a minor means of judging the value of his testimony. But this minor advantage is not regarded as essential, i.e., it may be dispensed with when it is not feasible. Cross-examination, however, the essential object of confrontation, remains indispensable. [at 28]

Wigmore then explains the meaning of confrontation:

> There is, however, a secondary advantage to be obtained by the personal appearance of the witness; the *judge* and the *jury* are enabled to obtain the elusive and incommunicable evidence of a witness' deportment while testifying, and a certain subjective moral effect is produced upon the witness.

. . . .

197 N. J. Super.

State v. Sheppard.
Cite as, 197 N. J. Super. 411

This secondary advantage, however, does not arise from the confrontation of the *opponent* and the witness; it is not the consequence of those two being brought face to face. It is the witness' presence before the *tribunal* that secures this secondary advantage—which might equally be obtained whether the opponent was or was not allowed to cross-examine. In other words, this secondary advantage is a result accidentally associated with the process of confrontation, whose original and fundamental object is the opponent's cross-examination. [§ 1395 at 153–154]

This opinion is underlined in the following note:

The following are instances of amusing legal pedantry: *Bennett v. State,* 62 *Ark.* 516, 36 *S. W.* 947 (1896) (holding erroneous the action of the trial court in proceeding with the examination of witnesses during the accused's absence in the water closet); *State v. Mannion,* 19 *Utah* 505, 57 *Pac.* 542 (1899) (a witness for the state claiming to be afraid of the defendant, the court placed him back in the room, out of sight and hearing of the witness; held improper, on the absurd ground that the dictionaries define "confront" as meaning 'to bring face to face' . . . [§ 1399 at 199]

The numerous exceptions to our hearsay rules, *Evid. R.* 63(1), *et. seq.,* present daily instances of testimonial admissions without any confrontation with the witness. In *Ohio v. Roberts, supra,* the court said that to give the confrontation clause an unqualified scope "would abrogate virtually every hearsay exception. . . ." 448 *U.S.* at 63, 100 *S. Ct.* at 2537.

Numerous cases reflect the use of electronic devices for the presentation of evidence and implicate the confrontation clause. *Benfield* has been cited above. In our own State, a defendant in a custody case excluded from a judge's private interview with a child, was permitted to hear the interview in the courtroom through an audio arrangement. The judge solicited questions from counsel

State v. Sheppard.   *197 N. J. Super.*
Cite as, 197 N. J. Super. 411

in the courtroom and repeated them to the child in his chambers. The technique was approved on appeal. *N.J. Youth and Family Services v. S.S.*, 185 *N.J. Super.* 3 (1982). The court held that the confrontation clause had not been violated. It said:

> We are satisfied that under the circumstances the procedure utilized was in the best interests of the child. It is evident from the record that the child was emotionally disturbed. The trial judge described him as 'rigid.' We conclude that the judge reasonably found that a certain degree of privacy would be more likely to elicit a genuine and reliable response from the child. We are satisfied that the trial judge acted reasonably in balancing the needs of the child for protection as against defendant's need to see her child when that child answered the judge's questions or answered questions submitted by the attorneys for cross-examination. . . .
>
> The use of the tape recorder and voice transmission under these circumstances is an acceptable method of balancing the interests of the child and the rights of the parties while at the same time affording the trier of fact maximum opportunity to ascertain the truth by questioning the child and observing his demeanor. [at 7]

N.J. Youth and Family Services cited *Kansas City v. McCoy*, 525 *S.W.* 2d 336 (Mo. Sup. Ct. 1975), with approval. In that case an expert witness testified against defendant via closed circuit television. On appeal defendant argued that his right of confrontation had been violated. The court, quoting *Douglas v. Alabama, supra*, said that "an adequate opportunity for cross-examination may satisfy the clause even in the absence of physical confrontation." *Id.* at 338. It held that the television arrangement provided the cross-examination opportunity required by the *Douglas* court; television did not significantly affect the ability to question and observe the witness. *Id.* at 339. Jury impact was found to be little different, whether the witness appeared in court, in person or by television. *Ibid.*

The conclusion is supported by *People v. Moran,* 114 *Cal. Rptr.* 413, 420, 39 *Cal. App.* 3d 398, 410 (Dist. Ct. App. 1974). In *Moran,* defendant argued that the jury could not weigh the credibility of a witness whose testimony at a preliminary hearing was presented at trial by videotape. The court held, however, that the jury could adequately weigh credibility and that "the process does not significantly affect the flow of information to the jury." It satisfied the "broad purposes" of the confrontation clause. 114 *Cal. Rptr.* at 420, 39 *Cal. App.* 3d at 410–411.

Moran also considered the use of videotape as a reliable medium for the presentation of evidence. It said:

> We turn next to defendant's due process contentions concerning the technical distortions of the medium and its failure to accurately transmit the demeanor of the witness and the dramatic components of the testimony. In general, the advantages and disadvantages of the "filtering" effect of the medium fall equally on both sides. Therefore, its use is "fair" and there is no inherent unfairness. Conceding that testimony through a television set differs from live testimony, the process does not significantly affect the flow of information to the jury. Videotape is sufficiently similar to live testimony to permit the jury to properly perform its function. Fair new procedures that facilitate proper factfinding are allowable, although not traditional. In any event, we do not comprehend defendant's contention that the tape is less valid or less reliable than the reading of the written transcript of the preliminary hearing. . . . the videotape is a modern technique that better protects the rights of all concerned. We can also take judicial notice of the fact of the ubiquity of television sets, as revealed by the 1970 census [96% of all households had at least one black and white television set], and recent availability of low-cost television cameras. With such a widespread availability of television comes a familiarity with its technical characteristics and distortions. Indeed the television camera is a stranger only in the slower moving apparatus of justice. [at 114 *Cal Rptr.* 420; citations omitted]

State v. Sheppard.   *197 N. J. Super.*
Cite as, 197 N. J. Super. 411

The federal courts have approved the use of a videotaped confession as evidence. In *Hendricks v. Swenson,* 456 *F.* 2d 503 (8 Cir. 1972), cited in *Moran,* the court said:

> If a proper foundation is laid for the admission of a videotape by showing that it truly and correctly depicted the events and persons shown and that it accurately reproduced the defendants' confession, we feel that it is an advancement in the field of criminal procedure and a protection of defendants' rights. We suggest that to the extent possible, all statements of defendants should be so preserved.

[3] In discussing videotapes as evidence, *Moran* held that the *California Evidence Code* § 250 included them in its definition of "writing," saying that its Legislature "recognized the widespread use of videotape in our society and its relevance to legal proceedings." 114 *Cal. Rptr.* 418, 39 *Cal. App.* 3d at 409. The rules in New Jersey can be read no differently. *Evid R.* 1(13) is nearly identical to the California rule. It provides:

> "Writing" means handwriting, typewriting, printing, photostating, photography, and every other means of recording upon any tangible thing, any form of communication or representation, including letters, words, pictures, sounds, or symbols, combinations thereof, provided that such recording is (a) reasonably permanent and (b) readable by sight.

Videotape records obviously fall within the language of the definition; they provide a means for recording words and pictures. Motion pictures have long been admissible in evidence in our courts. *Balian v. General Motors,* 121 *N.J. Super.* 118, 125 (App. Div. 1972). There is little difference between a motion picture presentation or a videotaped presentation except that the latter can provide the simultaneous photographing and transmission of information while the former cannot.

Our rules recognize the adequacy of videotaped evidence. *R.* 4:14-9, adopted in 1980, permits the taking and use of videotaped depositions in civil proceedings. *R.* 3:13-2 permits the taking and use of the deposition of a material witness who "may be unable to attend . . . as provided in civil actions. . . ." Thus, the videotaped deposition of a material witness may be introduced in evidence in our criminal courts. In addition to this formal authorization, it is apparent to this court from the demonstration of the equipment to be used in this matter and the expert testimony that the use of a videotaped presentation has the capacity to present clear, accurate, and evidentially appropriate transmissions of images and sounds to defendant, the judge, the jury, and the public.

[4] Great harm befalls the victims of child abuse. It destroys lives and damages our society. Known abusers are not being prosecuted because evidence against them cannot be presented. Children who are prevailed upon to testify may be more damaged by their traumatic role in the court proceedings than they were by their abuse. These considerations must be weighed and balanced against the right of confrontation in child abuse cases.

Any zeal for the prosecution of these cases, however, cannot be permitted to override the constitutional rights of the defendants involved. They are at great disadvantage in these cases. The testimony of a small child can be very winsome. (More winsome, perhaps, if she testifies in person than by videotape.) The difficulty of cross-examining a young child may prevent the exposure of inaccuracies. The charge of child abuse carries its own significant stigma. Defendants in these cases may find themselves ostracized, whether they are guilty or not. Like children, they too have ambivalent feelings and may decide, even though they believe they will be acquitted, that it is better for the child, the family and themselves to accept a plea agreement than to subject everyone involved to a trial. These problems must also be weighed in deciding the dimensions of the constitutional right of confrontation.

[5] The Confrontation Clause is not implacable in its demands. Nearly every authority agrees that it is subject to

exceptions. In reaching the conclusion, as this court has, that the use of videotaped testimony in this case of child abuse is permissible, it is accepted as a fact that only a modest erosion of the clause, if any, will take place. The child, through the use of video, will not be obliged to see the defendant or to be exposed to the usual courtroom atmosphere. Nevertheless, the defendant as well as the judge, the jury, and the spectators, will see and hear her clearly. Adequate opportunity for cross-examination will be provided. This is enough to satisfy the demands of the confrontation clause. If it is not, it represents a deserved exception. It is more than Wigmore would require. Everything but "eyeball-to-eyeball" confrontation will be provided. No case has held eye contact to be a requirement. It is not demanded when a witness "confronts" a defendant in the courtroom. No court rule requires eye contact and courtroom distances sometimes make such contact impossible. *Benfield* required face-to-face confrontation but did not define that requirement as including eye contact. To the extent that *Benfield* would deny the opportunity to use video equipment as proposed in the present case, I am in disagreement with its conclusions.

The child in the present case said that she *could* testify. The probable and possible consequences of that testimony, however, could not have been known to her. Indeed, her willingness to testify was grounded upon fear and misconception. She believed her stepfather would kill her for revealing his abuse and felt that she would be safe only if he went to jail. She thought, erroneously, that he would be sent to jail only if she testified in court. The risk her face-to-face testimony imposes is too great to be permitted. The concern which the court must have for her, and for all children, dictates a different course, when that course will not significantly impair the rights of the defendant.

In *Ohio v. Roberts, supra,* the Court "recognized that competing interests, if 'closely examined,' may warrant dispensing with confrontation at trial." 448 *U.S.* at 64, 100 *S. Ct.* at 2538. *N.J. Youth and Family Services, supra,* 185 *N.J. Super,* at 7, is to the same effect. *See also Chambers v. Mississippi,* 410 *U.S.* 284,

---

197 N. J. Super.   State v. Sheppard.
                          Cite as, 197 N. J. Super. 411

295, 93 *S. Ct.* 1038, 1045, 35 *L. Ed.* 2d 297 (1973). Child abuse
cases present such interests. The growing awareness of the social
consequences of child abuse has resulted in the enactment of
significant criminal statutes and has been underlined by our
Supreme Court in *State v. Hodge,* 95 *N.J.* 369 (1984):

> Crime within the family is one of the most deeply
> troubling aspects of contemporary life. Governor Kean recently
> established a task force to study the problem of child abuse.
> The United States Attorney General has instituted a Task Force
> on Family Violence to study the national dimensions of this
> problem. The Legislature has therefore graded sexual crimes
> that occur within the family differently from those occurring
> in other contexts. When criminal sexual conduct involves a
> victim who is 'at least 13 but less than 16 years old,' and
> the 'actor is a foster parent, a guardian, or stands in loco
> parentis within the household,' *N.J.S.A.* 2C:14-2(a)(2)(c), even
> though there may have been no force, the silent abuse inflicted
> deeply threatens the fabric of society. Accordingly, the
> Legislature graded this crime as one of the first degree. *N.J.S.A.*
> 2C:14-2(a). [at 377]

Truth is the ultimate quest. This is the proper interest of the
prosecution, the defense, the jury, the judge and all of our society
in all judicial proceedings. Philosophically, it may be argued that
truth is not an absolute. If so, that conclusion does not diminish
the premise. Truth, though unattainable in all of its labyrinthic
extremities, must always be the judicial goal. It is the purpose
undergirding our rules of evidence. *Evid. R.* 5 most appropriately
in the present setting, provides:

> The adoption of these rules shall not bar the growth
> and development of the law of evidence in accordance with
> fundamental principles to the end that the truth may be fairly
> ascertained.

State v. Sheppard.   *197 N. J. Super.*
Cite as, 197 N. J. Super. 411

In the present case, it is the opinion of the State's forensic psychiatrist that the video presentation of the child victim's testimony will enhance, not diminish, the prospect of obtaining the truth. His reasons for reaching that conclusion are convincing. The ambivalent position in which the child must find herself, her fear, guilt, and anxiety, become doubly oppressive when she is subjected to the courtroom atmosphere. Those factors become less burdensome through the use of video. "Proving Parent-Child Incest: Proof at Trial Without Testimony in Court by the Victim," 15 *U. of Mich. Journal of Law Reform* 131 (1981), corroborates this conclusion:

> Making the child incest victim testify in court has another distinct failing: it produces unreliable evidence. The trier of fact in an incest case faces a dilemma. Its determination of whether abuse occurred rests primarily upon the testimony of the child victim, but child witnesses are widely acknowledged to be unhelpful. They have a subjective sense of time, an inaccurate memory—especially with regard to experience such as incest which are repeated over time, and limited ability to communicate what they do not understand and recall. These natural disabilities tend to intensify when the child is afraid or under emotional stress as a child may regress to a less mature state or withdraw entirely. Incest victims are especially likely to suffer from these disabilities because they are young and find current pretrial and courtroom procedures especially traumatic. [at 137]

. . . .

The incest victim, unlike the witness to intrafamilial violence or the victim of physical abuse, is not only the child of the defendant nor merely his adversary witness, but also his accomplice. Her confusion and sense of guilt at her involvement is thus potentially far greater than other victim's

experience. It seems the trauma to the parent-child incest victim
is greater, her usefulness as a witness is less; the victim is
likely to have positive ties to the perpetrator; and other family
members are likely to be involved. No other case, however
similar in some respects, shares all of these complicating
factors. [at 142–151]

Thus, the use of video which enhances the quality of a child victim's
testimony, serves the essential demand for truth while satisfying
the constitutional mandate.

C.   The Court's Control of Cross-Examination.

[6,7] Confrontation's central purpose is provision of the
opportunity for cross-examination. *Douglas v. Alabama, supra.*
Like the right of confrontation, however, the right of cross-
examination is not without limitations. "The trial court has broad
discretion in determining the proper limitations of cross-
examination of a witness whose credibility is in issue." *State v.
Cranmer,* 134 *N.J. Super.* 117, 122 (App. Div. 1975); *State v. Pontery,*
19 *N.J.* 457, 472–473 (1955); *State v. Zwillman,* 112 *N.J. Super.*
6, 17–18 (App. Div. 1970), certif. den. 57 *N.J.* 603 (1971).

In the present case, there is, in fact, no curtailment of cross-
examination, only a restriction upon the means of transmitting
questions and answers. That restrictive action is less significant
than the action taken in *State v. Cranmer.* In that case, a defendant
charged with impairing the morals of an eight-year-old boy, who
became so emotionally distressed during cross-examination that
he could not continue, was denied any opportunity for further
cross-examination. The Appellate Division held that the
circumstances permitted the limitation upon cross-examination and
did not improperly abridge the right of confrontation. In *United
States v. Toliver, supra,* the court permitted the State's testimony
to continue in the absence of an ill defendant. The action was
affirmed on the ground that the evidence was not consequential.
The use of video equipment is less consequential. Its use may
be permitted as the discretionary action of the trial court in this
case.

State v. Sheppard.   *197 N. J. Super.*
Cite as, 197 N. J. Super. 411

D. Waiver of the Right of Confrontation.
The State argues that defendant has waived his right of
confrontation by threatening to kill the child victim if she revealed
his activities. In addressing this issue, it is assumed, *arguendo*,
that a videotaped presentation will not satisfy the requirements
of the confrontation clause. The court also adopts the conclusion
that the child cannot testify in court without risking serious
emotional damage. Finally, the court takes the position that a waiver
may occur even though the child is an available witness who can
testify but should not because of the risk involved. That risk, in
short, is one to which a child victim in a sexual abuse case should
not be subjected and, consequently, one which cannot be imposed
as a means of defeating a waiver claim.

[8] A defendant may waive his Sixth Amendment right of
confrontation. *United States v. Carlson, F.* 2d 1346, 1358 (8 Cir.
1976), *cert.* den. 431 *U.S.* 914, 97 *S. Ct.* 2174, 53 *L. Ed.* 2d 224
(1977). In *Carlson*, a witness testified before a grand jury but refused
to testify at trial. F.B.I. agents then testified, based upon
conversations with the witness, that his refusal was the result of
threats made by defendant. For this reason the grand jury testimony
of the witness was admitted into evidence. The Court of Appeals
affirmed the trial court's ruling that defendant had waived his right
of confrontation, saying "the sixth amendment does not stand as
a shield to protect the accused from his own misconduct or
chicanery." 547 *F.* 2d at 1359. It concluded that public policy was
served by a rule permitting the admission of an out-of-court
statement by a witness who has been intimidated by a defendant.

In *United States v. Balano,* 618 *F.* 2d 624 (10 Cir. 1979), *cert.*
den. 449 *U.S.* 840, 101 *S. Ct.* 118, 66 *L. Ed.* 2d 47 (1980), the court
said: "under the common law principle that one should not profit
by his own wrong, coercion can constitute voluntary waiver of
the right of confrontation." It added:

> We recognize that often the only evidence of coercion
> will be the statement of the coerced person, as repeated by
> government agents. Consequently, a reasonable doubt standard

for admission might well preclude a finding of waiver, no matter how reprehensible the defendant's conduct. On the other hand, we do not wish to emasculate the Confrontation Clause merely to facilitate government prosecutions. Thus, a prima facie showing of coercion is not enough. We hold, therefore, that before permitting the admission of grand jury testimony of witnesses who will not appear at trial because of a defendant's alleged coercion, the judge must hold an evidentiary hearing in the absence of the jury and find by a preponderance of the evidence that the defendant's coercion made the witness unavailable. [at 629]

The Court of Appeals found that the waiver determination was supported by "sufficient evidence." The trial court heard the testimony of the witness himself who, while refusing to discuss his reasons for not testifying, reiterated the truthfulness of his grand jury testimony. An FBI agent then testified to his conversations with the witness, indicating the circumstances surrounding various threats made against him by or on behalf of the defendant, if he testified, and his resulting fear. This was held to be sufficient evidence to support the claim of waiver.

In *Black v. Woods*, 651 *F.* 2d 528 (8 Cir. 1981), *cert.* den. 454 *U.S.* 847, 102 *S. Ct.* 164, 70 *L. Ed.* 2d 134 (1981), a witness refused to testify in a murder trial because she was afraid of being killed by defendant. Defendant had arranged a prior killing of another witness to prevent her from testifying against him in a robbery case. The murder witness was put on the stand by the prosecution but refused to testify and was held in contempt. The circuit court opinion does not set forth the evidence received at the trial level on the waiver question, but states:

> We agree with the state court that Black forfeited his confrontation right by a pattern of conduct that resulted in Link's fear which we find to be reasonable under the circumstances. The record is replete with Black's threats and attempts to intimidate against Link and others. Black had

physically abused Link and threatened to kill her if she did not do what she was told. [651 *F.* 2d at 531]

The court rejected the argument that there was no evidence of an express threat addressed to Link by Black, or anyone acting on his behalf, saying that the argument "ignores the facts of the case and the demonstrated tendencies of Black." It approved a comment of the Minnesota Supreme Court that Black's motive for killing the witness in the robbery case, namely, to assure himself of her silence, "provided Link with the most graphic and explicit threat possible if she testified against him." *Id.* at 532.

In the case at bar, the evidence of the defendant's threat to kill the child victim is hearsay. It consists of the victim's statement to Doctor Sadoff as repeated by him at the pretrial hearing. It is not admissible if the *Rules of Evidence* apply.

[9, 10] The question presented at the pretrial hearing was whether videotaped testimony of the victim would be admissible in evidence. The objection to its admission was based upon the claim that it would violate the Confrontation Clause. One answer to this claim is that the right of confrontation was waived by the defendant by reason of his threat. If there was a waiver, the videotaped testimony would be admissible without consideration of that right.

Evid. R. 8(1) states in part:

> When the . . . admissibility of evidence . . . is stated in these rules to be subject to a condition, and the fulfillment of the condition is in issue, that issue is to be determined by the judge. In his determination the rules of evidence shall not apply except for *R.* 4 or a valid claim of privilege.

Under this rule hearsay evidence is admissible for the purpose of making the *R.* 8(1) decision. *State v. Moore*, 158 *N.J. Super.* 68 (App. Div. 1978); *Hill v. Cochran*, 175 *N.J. Super.* 542 (App. Div. 1980). The hearsay evidence of Doctor Sadoff is therefore admissible, provided *Evid. R.* 8(3) does not apply. That rule provides in part:

---

197 N. J. Super.   State v. Sheppard.
                          Cite as, 197 N. J. Super. 411

Where by virtue of any rule of law a judge is required
in a criminal action to make a preliminary determination
as to the admissibility of a statement by the defendant, the
judge shall hear and determine the question of its admissibility
out of the presence of the jury. In such a hearing the *Rules
of Evidence* shall apply and the burden of proof as to
admissibility of the statement is on the prosecution.

Without more, this provision would require the *Rules of Evidence*
to be applied and Doctor Sadoff's testimony would be excluded.
It is apparent, however, from a reading of *Evid. R.* 8(3) in its entirety,
that it does not apply. The balance of that rule reads as follows:

If the judge admits the statement, he shall not inform
the jury that he has made a finding that the statement is
admissible, and he shall instruct the jury that they are to
disregard the statement if they find it is not credible. If the
judge subsequently determines from all of the evidence that
the statement is not admissible, he shall take appropriate
action.

It therefore appears that *Evid.R.* 8(3) is applicable only when the
"admissibility of a statement by the defendant" is a statement which
is intended to be introduced *at the trial.* That was not the purpose
of the hearing in the present case. The evidence of the threat to
kill was introduced only for the purpose of supporting the claim
of waiver, not for trial purposes. Consequently, *Evid. R.* 8(3) does
not apply. Neither do the *Rules of Evidence*, except *Evid. R.* 4
and rules relating to privilege.

This conclusion is supported by *U.S. v. Mastrangelo*, 693 F.
2d 269 (2 Cir. 1982). In that case grand jury testimony of a witness
was accepted into evidence after the witness had been killed while
on his way to testify. The court, citing *Carlson* and *Balano* as
well as numerous other cases, held that the misconduct of a defendant
could constitute a waiver of the Confrontation Clause. It said:

State v. Sheppard.   *197 N. J. Super.*
Cite as, 197 N. J. Super. 411

Since *Mastrangelo's* possible waiver of his sixth amendment right is a preliminary question going to the admissibility of evidence, the hearing will be governed by *Fed. R. Evid.* 104(a), which states that the exclusionary rules, excepting privileges, do not apply to such proceedings. Thus, hearsay evidence, including Bennett's grand jury testimony, will be admissible, as will all other relevant evidence. [at 273]

United States v. Thevis, 665 *F.* 2d 616 (5 Cir. 1982), *cert.* den. 459 *U.S.* 825, 103 *S. Ct.* 57, 74 *L. Ed.* 2d 61 (1982) is to the same effect. The evidence rule was not mentioned in *Carlson* or *Balano* or *Black,* all of which decided the waiver issue, however, on the basis of hearsay testimony. It is apparent that they relied upon the same approach.

It might be asserted that what is sought is not to determine the "admissibility of evidence," but rather to decide the manner of production of that evidence. It could be said that what is to be resolved is not whether the statement of the child victim is to be admitted, but rather to decide whether that statement is to be established by in-court testimony or by videotaped proofs. The difference is vital: If the concern is the manner of production of evidence as opposed to its basic admissibility *Evid. R.* 8(1) does not apply. That rule pertains only to issues concerning "the qualification of a person to be witness, or the admissibility of evidence, or the existence of a privilege." If *Evid. R.* 8(1) is not applicable, the hearsay evidence of the defendants' threat to kill is not admissible. The threat could then be proved only if the child victim appeared in court and testified against the defendant. This would be self-defeating. It would vitalize the unacceptable: permitting the defendant to gain advantage by his reprehensible conduct. This interpretation of *Evid. R.* 8(1) would thwart the truth. The *Rules of Evidence* as stressed by *Evid. R.* 5, are designed for the opposite purpose.

[11] Doctor Sadoff's testimony is therefore admissible. One problem remains: What is the burden of proof in the waiver hearing?" *Balano* held that waiver might be shown by a

197 N. J. Super.	State v. Sheppard.
	Cite as, 197 N. J. Super. 411

"preponderance of the evidence." 618 *F.* 2d at 629. *Thevis* required "clear and convincing" evidence. 665 *F.* 2d at 631. *Mastrangelo* adopted the preponderance of evidence test but remanded the case for a further hearing on the waiver question, instructing the trial judge to make findings under the clear and convincing standard as well. The court discussed the proof issue in the following language:

> [T]he Supreme Court precedents are mixed. While the Court has held the preponderance of evidence test applicable to suppression hearings involving possible misconduct by the government, *Lego v. Twomey*, 404 *U.S.* 477, 489, 92 *S. Ct.* 619, 626, 627, 30 *L. Ed.* 2d 618 (1972) (voluntariness of confession); *United States v. Matlock*, 415 *U.S.* 164, 177-78, 94 *S. Ct.* 988, 996, 997, 39 *L. Ed.* 2d 242 (1974) (consent to search), it has applied the clear and convincing standard to questions of admissibility involving constitutional requirements going to the reliability of evidence, *United States v. Wade*, 388 *U.S.* 218, 240, 87 *S. Ct.* 1926, 1939, 18 *L. Ed.* 2d 1149 (1967) (circumstances surrounding identification at a showup).
>
> These decisions are thus not dispositive. Since the right of confrontation is closely related to the reliability of testimonial evidence, the clear and convincing test may well apply to issues of admissibility arising under it. However, waiver by misconduct is an issue distinct from the underlying right of confrontation and not necessarily governed by the same rules concerning burden of proof. We see no reason to impose upon the government more than the usual burden of proof by a preponderance of the evidence where waiver by misconduct is concerned. Such a claim of waiver is not one which is either unusually subject to deception or disfavored by the law. Compare *McCormick, McCormick's Handbook on the Law of Evidence* § 340 (2d ed. 1972). To the contrary, such misconduct is invariably accompanied by tangible evidence such as the disappearance of the defendant, disruption

State v. Sheppard.   *197 N. J. Super.*
Cite as, 197 N. J. Super. 411

in the courtroom or the murder of a key witness, and there
is hardly any reason to apply a burden of proof which might
encourage behavior which strikes at the heart of the system
of justice itself. [693 *F.* 2d at 273]

[12]   In deciding whether the rule is to be "preponderance" or
"clear and convincing" in present circumstances, we must weigh
once again the confrontation right of the defendant against the
"right" of a child victim to testimonial protection. It has been
decided above that there is no absolute right of confrontation, that
the videotaped testimony of the child victim in a sexual abuse
case is admissible, either because it does not violate the
Confrontation Clause or because it represents a very modest
exception to that right. The purpose of the *R.* 8 hearing therefore
does not deal with an absolute constitutional mandate. Further,
since the hearing may be said to involve, indirectly, the reliability
of the videotaped evidence, reliability is enhanced by the minimal
incursion, if any, into the confrontation clause. It was the opinion
of Doctor Sadoff, corroborated by other authorities, that the video
presentation would be more likely than in-court testimony to
produce the truth. As in *Mastrangelo*, this court sees "no reason
to impose upon the government more than the usual burden of
proof by a preponderance of the evidence where a waiver by
misconduct is concerned."

[13]   Applying that test here, I conclude that the State has
supported the claim of waiver by sufficient evidence. The statement
of the child to the psychiatrist was made in a setting of confidence.
It was not made because the child knew that her statement could
effect a waiver of the Confrontation Clause. On the contrary, it
was the basis for her mistaken willingness to testify in court. It
was the opinion of Doctor Sadoff that the child's fear, occasioned
by the threat, was real. He also found that she was capable of
telling the truth. No contradictory testimony was presented by the
defendant. Under the circumstances, the proofs support the claim
of waiver. The Confrontation Clause is not available to the
defendant.

E. Conclusion.
The use of videotaped testimony of the child victim in this case will be permitted because:

   (a) It will not unduly inhibit the defendant's right of confrontation and therefore does not violate our constitutional provisions.
   (b) The testimony of a child victim in a child sexual abuse case may be presented by videotape as an exception to the confrontation requirement.
   (c) The use of the video technique is a permissible restriction of cross-examination.
   (d) The defendant in this case has waived his right of confrontation.

The videotaped presentation shall be subject to the conditions set forth in the schedule annexed to this opinion.

Conditions Imposed on the Use of the Videotaped Presentation

1. The testimony of the child victim shall be taken in a room near the courtroom from which video images and audio information can be projected to courtroom monitors with clarity.
2. The persons present in the room from which the child victim will testify (testimonial room) shall consist, in addition to the child, only of the prosecuting and defense attorneys together with the cameraman.
3. The only video equipment to be placed in the testimonial room shall be the video camera and such tape recording equipment as may be appropriate to carry out the conditions herein set forth.
4. The courtroom shall be equipped with monitors having the capacity to present images and sound with clarity, so that the jury, the defendant, the judge, and the public shall be able to see and hear the witness clearly while she testifies. The following monitors are deemed to be satisfactory insofar as screen size is concerned: Jury—25″; public—18″; defendant—10″; judge—7″.

5. It shall not be necessary to conceal the video camera. A videotape shall be made containing all images and all sounds projected to the courtroom which tape shall be introduced in evidence as a state exhibit.

6. No bright lights shall be employed in the testimonial room.

7. Color images shall be projected to the courtroom by the video camera.

8. The video camera shall be equipped with a zoom lens to be used only on notice to counsel who shall have an opportunity to object.

9. The video camera, the witness and counsel shall be so arranged that all three persons in the testimonial room can be seen on the courtroom monitors simultaneously. The face of the witness shall be visible on the monitors at all times, absent an agreement by counsel or direction by the court for some other arrangement. The placement of counsel in the testimonial room shall be at the discretion of each counselor.

10. The defendant and his attorney shall be provided by the State with a video system which will permit constant private communication between them during the testimony of the child witness.

11. An audio system shall be provided connecting the judge with the testimonial room to the end that he can rule on objections and otherwise control the proceedings from the bench.

12. In the event testimony is being recorded by use of a mechanical system, the video monitors or one of them shall be so connected to that equipment as to record all of the child witness's testimony.

13. In the event the proceedings are being recorded by a court stenographer, that stenographer shall remain in the courtroom and shall rely upon the video monitors for the purpose of recording the testimony of the child victim.

14. All video equipment, the videotape and the cameraman, shall be provided by and at the expense of the State.

15. The oath of the child witness may be administered by the judge using the audio equipment, or by the court clerk who may enter the testimonial room for that purpose only, or otherwise as the judge may direct.

16. The testimony of the child victim shall be interrupted at reasonable intervals to provide the defendant with an opportunity for person-to-person consultation.

17. The trial court, before the child victim testifies, shall provide the jury with appropriate instructions concerning the videotape presentation.

18. These conditions have been adopted by the court after counsel has been provided with the opportunity to make objections to them.

INDEX